Dr. Lillian R. Dangott is an assistant professor at the Medical School, University of Nevada, Reno, where she teaches gerontology and holistic health. She has co-authored three books, published in numerous professional journals, and is in private practice.

Dr. Richard A. Kalish is presently on the faculty at the California School for Professional Psychology, Berkeley, California. He has written five previous books as well as over 125 articles.

Both Dr. Dangott and Dr. Kalish have consulted extensively with professional and private agencies.

Lillian R. Dangott / Richard A. Kalish

A TIME TO ENJOY
The Pleasures of Aging

A SPECTRUM BOOK

PRENTICE-HALL, INC., ENGLEWOOD CLIFFS, N.J. 07632

179
D182
cop. 1

Library of Congress Cataloging in Publication Data

Dangott, Lillian R
   A time to enjoy.

   (A Spectrum Book)
   Bibliography: p.
   Includes index.   Old age. — Psychology.
   1. Old age—United States. 2. Aging—Psychological
aspects. 3. Aged—Care and hygiene—United States.
I. Kalish, Richard A., joint author. II. Title.
HQ1064.U5D36   301.43'5   78-21873
ISBN 0-13-921692-8
ISBN 0-13-921684-7 pbk.

Editorial/production supervision and interior design by Norma Karlin
Cover design by Al Pisano
Manufacturing buyers: David Hetherington and Cathie Lenard

*This book is dedicated to the "pleasures of aging" shared with my daughters,
Andrea and Seana, and my husband, Jake.   LIL*

A Spectrum Book

Printed in the United States of America

10 9 8 7 6 5 4 3 2 1

Prentice-Hall International, Inc., *London*
Prentice-Hall of Australia Pty. Limited, *Sydney*
Prentice-Hall of Canada, Ltd., *Toronto*
Prentice-Hall of India Private Limited, *New Delhi*
Prentice-Hall of Japan, Inc., *Tokyo*
Prentice-Hall of Southeast Asia Pte. Ltd., *Singapore*
Whitehall Books Limited, *Wellington, New Zealand*

CONTENTS

FOREWORD

Western society has, for much too long, ignored the advantages and values of age. On this score, of course, we have much to learn from our Asian friends. There is considerable evidence that the length of life is affected more by an individual's expectations and desire to live, or unfortunately, sometimes, will to die, than by most other factors. As Dr. Dangott has pointed out, good health habits not only can extend life, but can enhance health and extend the usefulness of life.

An encouraging trend in this country is the move to abolish mandatory retirement at sixty-five years of age. When we consider that the biological expectations of life should allow the average human being to live somewhere between 120 and 150 years, radical changes must occur in the attitude of society as a whole toward the aging process. It seems obvious that the major factor is individual responsibility and choice. In other words, if you choose to be happy and healthy by following good health habits, then you can expect to extend your life possibly twice as long as the average American lives today. One of the startling reactions of many individuals, when faced with this fact, is "I don't want to live that long." My inclination, then, is to ask them how long they do want to live. It turns out that most people have such a bleak view of aging, they want to hurry and get life over with to avoid winding up being aged! It isn't just the fear of being debilitated or an invalid, but somehow the horror of suddenly finding oneself "old" that seems to worry many individuals.

Dr. Dangott's book should go a long way toward helping people to recognize that they have choices and to offer them an opportunity to take advantage of, and enjoy, the pleasures of aging. This is the kind of book that most people should read when they're twenty, and re-read every ten years for a reassessment each decade of goals, desires, and the will to live.

C. Norman Shealy, M.D., Ph.D.
President, American Holistic Medical Association

PREFACE

For too long, being old has been depicted as a tragedy. We are regaled with a lengthy list of how needy the elderly are, how poorly they are treated, and how much must be done for them. As obviously true as these needs are, it seems to us that the picture has been distorted. Aging is often defined entirely in terms of the sick and needy. By emphasizing the horrors of aging, we have looked only at ways of alleviating these horrors. As a result, the *benefits* of being older, the potential for growth in the later years, the possibilities for pleasure and satisfaction are all ignored.

We look at the other side of the picture—the positive, growth-related, *becoming* side of the coin. We do not paint a universally positive picture of aging, because aging has its difficulties. We do, however, call attention to both the benefits and the potentials of aging. We bring together ideas from humanistic psychology and holistic medicine to explore how aging can be different from the bleak picture usually painted.

We enjoyed working on this book, partially because it made us feel good about older people and good about the potentials of our own aging, we who are the not-yet-old. We hope you enjoy reading the book, also in part because it makes you feel good about older people in general and about yourself in particular.

In developing our ideas, we thought of several audiences, and we are optimistic enough to hope that we can reach them all. We want to reach people who are either elderly themselves or who are closely involved with the elderly—right there an amazingly large portion of the population. We also want to reach younger people who are open to raising questions about the traditional views of aging, the stereotypes that are mostly negative. And we want to reach middle-aged people, like us, who are in that awkward in-between age: too young to be old and too old to be young. That sounds like just about everybody, and we guess that is what we want to do.

We are "true believers" in our cause. We feel it is essential that you join us in recognizing, approving, and encouraging continued enjoyment and growth throughout life and the pleasures of aging.

I wish to acknowledge with gratitude the help I received from the following friends and colleagues: Bud Baldwin, Bill Hudspeth, and Sam Keen. Also, Jake Huber, Martin Dangott, and Shad Adamson.

One

THE POTENTIALS OF AGING

You have good reason to be optimistic about the quality of your life as you grow older! You have the potential to increase your total functioning, to expand the use of your creative energy for your own satisfaction, and to enable others to do the same. You can continue to learn, to redefine your potential capabilities, and to seek new meanings throughout life. Even when death is imminent, you do not need to give up the possibility of growth; you can often still make choices and have an impact on this last phase of life also.

The old concept of aging was a downhill path, beginning at 60 or 50 or even 40 or 30; it implied slow deterioration, accelerating with time. The new concept of aging dispels these grim inaccuracies. Instead of a single downhill path, there can be a network of paths, many going uphill; instead of accelerating deterioration, there can be the opportunity for extensive personal growth.

1

And life itself may become longer and healthier. The American Medical Association's Council on Medical Service states that conservatively speaking, with our *existing* knowledge, many more people should be able to live to the age of 90, 100, or longer (Winter, 1973). Dr. Alex Comfort (1961), a biologist well known for many years for his work in gerontology before his writing on human sexuality brought him fame, believes that people are fully capable of living to the age of 100, but that "Man has been killing himself prematurely for a long time by social, dietary, and political means [p. 122]." Little doubt exists among scientists from a variety of disciplines that aging as we know it today is not inevitable. Mammals, for example, live about six times as long as it takes them to complete their growth from infancy to maturity ("maturity" defined as full physical growth). Therefore, since humans reach physical maturity by about the age of 17, our life expectancy should be over 100 years!

Scientists are also critical of the popular misconception that "to be old is to be sick." Some biologists estimate that within a few decades the average 70-year-old could be as healthy as the average 40-year-old is today. In fact, most older people in the middle and upper classes are already enjoying basically good health. Good health in aging is often possible for those with the know-how (and financial resources) to take care of themselves.

Aging interests us all for very personal reasons. I grew up in an environment in which a woman growing old was rarely regarded as beautiful. "Old" meant anybody over thirty-five! The women I met who were fifty or older exuded a sense of futility; they seemed void of sensuality and sexuality, of adventurousness, of enthusiasm for their lives, and of involvement with the world. Most of them I rejected with dismay. How was I to look forward to my aging when the lives of older women seemed so barren and empty?

Because of such negative attitudes about aging, many people in this culture suffer from *gerontophobia*—a fear of growing old. Partly out of my own personal struggle with this affliction, I have scrutinized the research literature to determine alternatives to the familiar grim view of aging. I learned that there are startling contrasts among people in how they age. The popular belief that aging ushers in a uniformly massive decline in physical and psychological functioning has *no* support. In fact, a forty-year longitudinal study of over one hundred older Californians indicated that growing older can give individuals new opportunities for growth and well-being (Maas & Kuypers, 1974). However, since successful aging may depend as much on your expectations as it does on your health or financial means, you must think ahead and explore your own concepts of aging. What you expect to happen often determines the reality of what does happen.

PERSONAL PRECONCEPTIONS: WHAT WILL YOU BE LIKE?

At what age will you begin to consider yourself "older"? As an experiment, imagine yourself as older and then project your physical appearance. Begin by seeing yourself as 20 years older than you are. Then, project yourself into whatever age you view as "old." Imagine your face looking into a mirror. What is the texture of your skin? Where are the lines on your face? How have your eyes changed? Your hair? How is your appearance changed? What can you accept and what do you have trouble accepting?

Take a few minutes to check out how you feel in contemplating these changes. Many people feel anxious or sad; some people report being "resigned." Very few say that they welcome—or even accept—the physical changes of aging.

To develop your self-awareness, try responding to the questions that follow. Each question presents a different way of viewing your body. We will ultimately focus on your entire physical body, visualizing different qualities that you might assume when you are older.

First, picture your body as it is now, outside and inside.
. . . Now visualize yourself, in as much detail as possible, at
some specific age you consider to be "old"—knowing that your
self-images, fears, ideas, and expectations about aging can influence the way in which you actually age. Write down all
your responses, giving yourself as much time as you need.

Body Images

1. What is the strongest part of your body?
2. What is the weakest part?
3. What is the oldest part?
4. What is the youngest part?
5. What do you consider the most attractive part of your body?
6. What is the least attractive?
7. Where does your body have the most warmth?
8. Where is your body coldest?
9. What is the most vulnerable part of your body—the place most quickly or easily hurt?
10. What is the smoothest part of your body?
11. What is the roughest part?
12. What is the hardest part?
13. Where do you carry tensions in your body?
14. What part of your body do you most want to change?
15. What do you least want to change?
16. What part of your body are you ashamed of?
17. What part of your body do you feel most proud of?

Can you picture your "older" body as a whole, which is
at the same time made up of different components and qualities? As a result of our generalized, negative attitudes about
aging, we frequently condemn our total body, ignoring the
wide range of body qualities and feelings. The one-dimensional
concept of "old age" should not be allowed to subsume our
individual attributes.

Regardless of economic resources, you have surely noticed some older people stop caring about themselves; they seem to lack pride in who they are. They have a tendency to dress in a careless or sloppy manner; they are not as concerned with body cleanliness as they once were. The body-image fantasy exercise can help you counter a common defeatist assumption that to be old is to be unattractive. Being in touch with a variety of feelings about your body allows for a more positive self-image.

EXPECTATIONS

Can you imagine now not only your appearance, but also what your life will be like when you are old? No one, of course, has a crystal ball, but we do have projections—anticipations of our wishes and anxieties. In recognizing our expectations, fears, and images about aging, we are in a position to influence positively what will happen. Explore your thoughts about some of the following questions:

1. What personality qualities do you most like to see in old people?
2. What do you most fear about growing older? What is the worst thing that can happen to you in old age?
3. Would you like to retire? At what age? Will you have a choice? How do you feel about retirement? What do you picture your economic situation to be?
4. What kind of housing would you like? What kind of neighborhood do you want? What kind of community?
5. How will you like to spend your leisure time? What kinds of activities do you expect to find pleasurable?
6. What changes do you expect in your sexuality?
7. What will be the quality of your friendships? Will you make new friends easily? (Who would you like for your friends?)
8. What do you imagine your health will be like when you are old? What health problems do you anticipate?
9. What advantages do you see in being old? What kinds of pleasures are more possible in your later years than in your youth?

SELF-FULFILLING PROPHECIES
AND NEW OPTIONS

"You are as old as you feel" is a truism. But a more precise statement might be: "You are as old as you expect to be."

Though we rarely dwell on our expectations, they can govern our strategies in life with great effect. We often live with a time schedule about when and how things should happen. Our expectations, of which we are often only dimly aware, may not even be commensurate with what we really want. Yet they sit inside us, waiting in our minds like old familiar pieces of furniture, seen but not recognized. Anticipation can therefore evolve into reality.

Aging occurs so gradually, so subtly, that we can almost deny its existence. We attend to the phenomena of aging only when we are faced with the measures of passing time: birthdays, reunions, old photographs, and so on. Though we can deny our age, we live according to an internal timetable of when things should occur. These expectations usually have an age referent. For example, we often feel that there is a "time" for marrying and a "time" for having children . . . and yet, the *right* "time" is precisely when we make them happen!

When the "time" comes for us to grow old, we become fearful.

> *Everyman desires to live long,*
> *but no man would be old.*

> —Jonathan Swift[1]

For most people, self-sufficiency and independence are extremely important qualities of life. Both men and women say that what they most fear about old age is the possibility of being helpless, poor, sick, dependent, and unable to care for themselves (Harris, 1975). Poor health is something we all dread, and for some people it represents a condition worse than

[1] From *Thoughts on Various Subjects* (1711).

death. But in the absence of chronic poor health, why should growing older be an ordeal?

Too often we adopt stereotypes of aging from the sick and the needy, rather than from the healthy and successful. Many people associate old age with the expectation that they will be incapacitated. Unfortunately, this myth of inevitable decrepitude can invite or create the situation. If you expect to be in poor health, you may fail to take care of yourself—thus fulfilling your own prophecy. The paradox of self-fulfilling prophecies is that when you are caught in one, you usually do not know it (Wilmot, 1975). Hence, self-awareness and consciousness of our expectations become all the more important.

> Age stereotypes serve as self-fulfilling prophecies. To expect life to grow sad and thin after 60, to expect no new consuming interest after 50, to expect one's sexuality to become less and less important and gratifying after 40 is usually to be proven right. Because in nothing is expectation so powerful as it is in the matter of growing older—a journey in which we paradoxically both need our guidebooks and need to put them aside.   *[Bridges, 1977, p. 68]*

Aging is not an inevitable circumstance that happens to us as passive recipients: It is a style of living that we create. We actively choose from a number of options that determine our health. We all must age; however, we need not grow "old" in the contemporary derogatory sense.

Though many of the current generation of older people project a grim image, we need not face a similar future. For example, a person who is now 65 was born when World War I was raging in Europe. Tremendous social and educational changes have taken place since then. According to 1975 Bureau of Census data, about 40 percent of Americans 55 years of age and older have completed no more than nine years of school. People born more recently have a higher level of education. They also have different life experiences, having been reared in a contemporary era of TV, jet travel, psychological sophistication, militant politics, and liberalized sexual attitudes. We are witnessing a transition toward a new concept of aging, toward a demand for a higher level of health, and toward the opportunity for greater personal growth.

LIFE DOES NOT GROW OLD

In the past, wisdom was a highly valued characteristic of aging. The older statesman, the tribal chief, the judge, the senior priest, the head of the family, the rich property owner, and the political leader all represented respected older citizens. These prestigious roles often imply, however, that in having attained the quality called "wisdom," a person arrives at a constant state. In this sense, wisdom is a stagnant quality, rather than a process of continuing growth and development.

Certain older people tend to preach and teach; they feel they should "know it all" in their old age—that they should be "wise." A new role model for aging could make it just as acceptable for older people to be seekers. An elderly person can still explore life, rather than believe he or she has the answer— "wisdom."

The fear of growing old can be so intense that people cling to the pseudo-symbols of youth, taking their clues on how to "be" from sources outside themselves. But, obviously, perpetual youth doesn't occur merely by adopting the external trappings of youth. Those who attempt to masquerade as much younger people in dress, language, or mannerism are demonstrating a desperate rigidity rather than the flexibility they so desire. In all probability, these people have stopped growing: With their focus fixed on the external, they are no longer developing their inner resources.

Growth can occur at all times of life. For many years, scientific studies of aging focused only on the decline; now researchers are turning to studies of the increased potentials that occur with aging. Current research suggests that human abilities can *improve* with age, as we will point out throughout this book.

In America, vast monetary resources are poured into the preparation of young people for adult roles, but little attention is given to preparing young people for their older-adult roles. Adult education programs in American colleges and adult schools have given virtually no attention to personal growth in late adulthood. This attitude is rapidly changing; we are seeing the birth of a new interest in "well-aging." With our increasing knowledge, individuals can minimize the supposed negative effects of aging.

The focus on growth helps to nurture a high level of wellness in aging. Renee Taylor (1964) has studied the people of Hunza (an area in Asia), where men and women live vigorous lives past a hundred years of age. The 80-year-old Hunza ruler has this to say about aging:

> The true keynote of life is growth, not aging. Life does not grow old. So-called age is the deterioration of enthusiasm, faith to live, and the will to progress.

Two

MYTHS OF AGING

To dispel myths, we must become more conscious of them. Almost unconsciously, we caricature the elderly on the narrow bases of our limited personal contact with them and of our stereotyped notions of them.

What are your suppositions about older people? Do you presuppose a certain type of personality, or a different kind of intelligence? How do you react when you meet someone who appears to be old? Many of us try to avoid older persons because we feel uncomfortable with them; we are also likely to feel impatient because we anticipate that the older person will move slowly or understand poorly. Does this describe you at all? The next time you meet a "senior citizen" try to observe what happens; increase your awareness of what "oldness" means to you.

Even before they speak, we identify older persons by their faces, hands, and physical bearing. They *look* different. And if their hearing is poor or their thoughts are slow, if their hands tremble or their step is hesitant, we are likely to judge them as a species apart from ourselves.

Of all life's realities, old age is the most difficult to imagine. We behave as if we will never grow old; we live as if we will never die. Both old age and death are abstractions of the future, difficult to grasp, mysteries of other people's lives. For many people, it is easier to imagine being dead than to imagine being old (de Beauvoir, 1973). Death is commonly conceptualized as a void, a transcendance to another state, a state of nonbeing, in which people imagine they retain their identities. For those who believe in immortality, a person's present identity either continues in death or changes according to how well the life was lived. But for many, being an old person means conceiving of one's self as a *different* person, a markedly changed being. Unlike death, old age means a mutation of the self, changes forced upon the healthy adult by the decay of body and mind. For this reason, most people avoid conceiving of themselves as being old (Golde & Kogan, 1959, p. 359).

STEREOTYPES OF OLD AGE

A 70-year-old woman was asked in an interview (Collier, 1975), "What do you encounter as the stereotypes of old age?"

"Oh, there are so many," she replied, "and older people believe them, and younger people are taught to expect them. Old people drool. They take laxatives all the time. Their sex organs are dried up. They can't understand youthful progress and are stuck in the past. Senility is judged an inevitable part of age [p. 29]."

The average person grows older within an emotional atmosphere riddled with myths and stereotypes about aging (Saul, 1974, p. 20). The old are generally thought to be "played out." Old age is looked upon as a period characterized by poor health, loneliness, resistance to change, failing mental powers, physical decay, economic insecurity, and dependency.

Stereotypes make your thinking rigid and oversimplified. References to "the elderly" imply common characteristics for a group of people based on their age. In reality, elderly individuals are no more alike than people of any age. The differences among individuals in any age group after infancy are more numerous than the similarities.

But the way that older people see themselves and the complexity of their needs are often different from what others would predict. In research done by Bennett and Eckman (1973), people of all ages were given sentences about older people to complete, a few of which are listed below. How would you complete them? (Take a moment to think about your responses so you can make comparisons with others.)

1. In general, old people need _____

   _____.

2. One of the greatest fears of many old people is _____

   _____.

3. Old people tend to resent _____

   _____.

4. One of the greatest pleasures of old people is _____

   _____.

Some of the results of the survey were surprising. For example:

1. In general, old people need—
   Younger people most often named *assistance* as the major need of old people. Older people cited their dominant need as wanting to be liked and valued by others.
2. One of the greatest fears of many old people is—
   Younger people said that death and dying were great fears,

while older people most often stressed a lack of money and financial insecurity. Death is not the primary fear of older people. Their fears are more immediate, reflecting realistic insecurity in regard to the opportunities available.

3. Old people tend to resent—
   Younger people guessed that the object of older people's resentments was younger people! The older people, specifically referring to their treatment by others, said they most resented rejection.

4. One of the greatest pleasures of old people is—
   Younger people judged that the greatest pleasure was in family, while older people more frequently chose companionship and love.

Although our stereotypes of old age are predominantly negative, virtually no studies follow people over the period of a lifetime to determine how their feelings change. Do people's attitudes necessarily grow more negative as they themselves age? Possibly the young person's dim view changes, becoming more positive as she or he approaches old age.

Many individuals have reported to me that the older they become, the happier they feel and the more fully they learn to live. However, unless they are in poor health, people rarely judge themselves as "old." "Old" usually refers to the way in which we see others. You may have heard your 84-year-old great aunt refer to her somewhat younger friends in a nursing home as "those old people."

In addition to aggravating our fear and denial of aging, existing stereotypes lead to what has been called "ageism." *Ageism* is discrimination and inequality based on hostile or negative attitudes toward the aged. It is similar to racism and sexism in that they are all attitudes and behaviors—either individual or institutionalized—that discriminate against people because of their age, race, or sex.

People do not generally recognize the magnitude of age inequality in our society. For example, compulsory retirement and other age discriminations in institutions are legal and taken for granted. Many professional schools, such as law, psychology and medicine, refuse applications from students over the age of 30 or 35. The rationale is that someone who has fewer years to serve in the profession as younger candidates is not as worth training. Underlining this dubious logic is the stereotypical assumption that students past a certain age are slow learners.

As long as we believe that older persons are poor, sick, rigid, unhappy, and incapable of learning, the prospect of old age is of course unattractive and repelling. In reaction to our own stereotypes, then, we dissociate ourselves from old people and relegate them to an inferior status in our society.

Stereotypes are difficult to dispel, even among supposedly objective professionals. Early research findings suggested that old age was a period of life marked by failing physical and mental powers, resistance to change, and rigidity of personality. These conclusions resulted from focusing, for the most part, on assessing age–related differences rather than on the origins and meaning of those differences. Another reason early research results supported stereotypes of old age is that few people think of old age as a time of health and growth, and researchers mirrored this attitude by focusing on instruments and scales to measure the deficiencies, losses, and declines that come with age.

Subsequent research is beginning to adjust this image. While we now know that many of our stereotypes are based more on fancy than fact, the results of newer studies are reaching the public much too slowly. And even with the positive findings of recent research, a major question remains unanswered: How much of what is observed in the aging process is the result of a self-fulfilling prophecy?

Stereotypes are self-fulfilling, because they are so much a part of us. To begin with, teaching stereotypes is part of the process of socialization. Children learn some of their attitudes toward old people and how to play the role of an old person through literature. An analysis of children's literature from the years 1870 to 1960 showed increasingly negative attitudes toward older people (Seltzer & Atchley, 1971). This study supports other findings that ageism has increased over the decades. While blacks, Chicanos, and women have long since taken action against the way they are portrayed in children's literature, older people are only now beginning to do so. *Stereotypes tend also to be self-perpetuating,* because they are so built-in. Simone de Beauvoir (1973) writes:

> If old people show the same desires, the same feelings, and the same requirements as the young, the world looks upon them with disgust: in them love and jealousy seem revolting or absurd, sexuality repulsive . . . they are required to be a standing example of all the virtues. Above all, they are called upon to display serenity. *[p.11]*

Ironically, in enacting their role of "serenity," the older people in our society rob themselves of their political power and of the possibility of raising their status through activism. In our society, institutions very often respond only to aggressive demands.

Research data indicate that old people are greatly concerned about being set apart, rejected, or considered different (Bennett & Eckman, 1973, p. 584). Certainly, the thinning hair or slowing speech of an older person tells only the surface story; but unfortunately, in the absence of real data, we often manufacture suppositions about what older people are experiencing—how they regard themselves, their lives, or their future. The pity is that we are not hearing the story of the elderly, the potential for them and our own old age. We are listening only to the nervous chatter of our own inner voices.

Our attitudes toward aging affect the lives of others as well as our own. Our distaste is communicated, causing older persons to view themselves negatively, resulting in a feedback loop that reinforces negative views in both young and old.

The most destructive aspect of what happened to blacks in American society was not the rampant bigotry on the part of whites, but the inevitable self-hate and self-stereotyping which slowly but surely wrapped tentacles around the black's psyche. For this reason, "Black is beautiful" was one of the most important concepts to come out of the Civil Rights Movement. As many blacks did prior to Civil Rights, most older people have accepted the "place" they have been assigned in society. As difficult as it may be to imagine, some day perhaps we will perceive that "Old is beautiful" too. Advertisers may then seek out old people, as well as young whites and blacks, for their symbols of beauty; they have already begun to include the "token" older person in their materials.

ORIGINS AND PERPETUATION OF STEREOTYPES

Our ideas about the aged are inherited from two different traditions: first, from the classic Greek view that aging is an unmitigated misfortune and tragedy, and second from the traditional Judeo-Christian view that old age is the summit of life and the pinnacle of wisdom. The latter supposition, permeating the Old Testament, was a role assigned to the early Biblical patriarchy. The dualism of our philosophical heritage is summarized in these contrasting statements about death: the ancient Hebrews believed, "The wicked die young"; the Greeks said, "Whom the gods love die young."

Obviously, the Greek cult of youth and its concomitant horror of old age dominate our culture. However, we regularly chastise ourselves for subscribing to this tradition: ministers, priests, and rabbis moralize against the pagan worship of youth, imploring us to respect our elders and provide for their needs. The "white man's burden" has been replaced by "youth's obligations." But whether we call it a burden or obligation, charity is an insult, a kind of assistance we dole out to those of inferior status.

In this day, mass communication is a significant vehicle for social change. Currently, television is the medium with the greatest impact on our culture (Ashmore, 1975, p. 19).

However, television perpetuates old age myths through stereotypic characterizations. Dr. David Peterson (1975), in a study of the television image of older people, reported that they are generally shown as ill, inflexible, old-fashioned, and feeble; they are portrayed in "old-fashioned clothing with yesterday's hairdo." Aronoff (1974) analyzed characters in television dramas from 1969 through 1971. He found that old people comprise less than 5 percent of characterizations, rarely fill major roles, and are most often depicted as victims or villains. The percentage of older people shown on television is less than half the number that actually exists in our population. This evidence reflects the apparent conviction of producers and script writers that interesting things happen only to young people (Davis, 1975, p. 322). Aronoff's study concluded that "Aging in prime time drama is associated with increasing evil, failure, and unhappiness . . . females age earlier and faster than males. Chances of male villainy increase with age" (Aronoff, 1974, p. 87).

Advertising, another powerful instrument of change, whether in television or other media, also falls short of doing the older person justice. Rarely does it show older people enjoying themselves or functioning in competent roles. In an analysis of eight popular women's magazines for April and May, 1975, only two ads featured older people: one showed an older woman scrubbing out an oven; the other pictured a group of older people enacting a traditional dinner in an ad for dishes (Dangott, 1975a).

Most television commercials in fact cater to the young, vivacious, and exciting. Barrages of youth-oriented commercials reinforce our emphasis on being young. For example, hair commercials show beautiful women surrounded by admiring young men; deodorant commercials picture young people who, because they are very active all day, need the extra "protection" of the product. Apparently, older people never shampoo their hair, brush their teeth, or use deodorant! The few types of commercials that consistently utilize older people are advertisements for pain pills, denture cleaners, hair dyes, and laxatives. In ads for rinses to cover the gray, old age seems to set in at about thirty.

Madison Avenue executives have decided, apparently, that

the older age group is not a lucrative source of purchasing power (Ashmore, 1975, p. 19), although they may be in the process of changing their minds. The older person's income is reduced, and, presumably, his or her need for material goods is largely satisfied. This attitude is reminiscent of the way in which the media viewed blacks as happy with their singing and religion, content to live without material goods. We tend to rationalize the existence of social outcasts in our society by saying that they are happy and content with their lives.

Television is sometimes the only friend of older people who are cut off by illness or isolation; it provides them with information and entertainment. So it is all the more unfortunate that television reinforces the negative stereotypes that older people have about themselves . . . and that all of us are offered such poor role models for our own aging.

If mass communication is failing to give us a true picture of older people and aging, what then are the facts about aging?

THE FACTS ABOUT AGING

Our popular stereotypes of aging, almost without exception, are not accurate. Some of the myth-exploding information now available is as follows:

1. Intelligence is relatively stable throughout life, unless the person is suffering from a health condition affecting her or his cognitive abilities. Sometimes heart or circulatory problems or even advanced cancer can reduce awareness or diminish mental activity. Most important, learning is possible at any age.
2. Physical activity can continue throughout a person's life. Certain kinds of activities can remain relatively constant. Lifestyle and environmental/cultural factors, rather than age, are primarily related to the amount of activity in a person's life.
3. Creativity can occur at any age.
4. Individuals with more education have better health and appear able to adapt more successfully.

5. Personality does not normally change drastically with aging: People show a consistency throughout life. When personality does change, the change is not directly the result of aging.
6. The sex drive and related behavior that often continue well into the eighties.
7. Age is a poor index of the differences between people in their abilities to find pleasure in living and to experience happiness.

Casual observation tells us that older people tend to function less well than younger people. We conclude, then, that people reach their peak, both mentally and physically, as young adults; from then on they go downhill, at first slowly, then more rapidly. Until recently, aging was studied according to this assumption. We compared older people with younger people at the same point in time, a method of study referred to as *cross-sectional.* For instance, a group in their twenties was compared with a group in their sixties. The assumption behind the cross-sectional study is that any difference found between age groups is due to age changes.

This assumption is incorrect. People of various ages differ in many ways and for many reasons other than a difference in ages. Most importantly, they belong to different generations: They have disparate life experiences and values, as well as different levels of education. When your grandparents reached the age of 30, they had experienced a much different history than you did (or will) by the same age; the world itself was different in their time.

Only recently have we seen results from *longitudinal studies* in which individuals are followed over periods of time to discover if changes occur. This different scientific approach has yielded an immense change in our conclusions about the process of aging. However, as you can imagine, longitudinal studies present many problems: They are difficult to conduct since they are so long-term; they are costly for the same reason; and they can saddle the investigator with outmoded research methods. Furthermore, such studies require the continuity of interested staff members who will maintain the project. Since people often move, sometimes die, or simply get bored with being "a subject," "drop-outs" also constitute a problem.

Perhaps the most problematic aspect of longitudinal studies is sorting out which changes in function are due to age and thereby characteristic of others in general, and which are due to unique events in the life of an individual and thereby irrelevant to aging. For example, a series of small strokes can be an intervening event that may cause a drop in intelligence: Such a change is due not to age but to illness, and it should not be generalized as a normal part of aging. Yet it is more likely to become a possibility in the later years of a person's life.

Our new findings from longitudinal studies clash with previous cross-sectional studies, which showed that intelligence decreased with age. During the past several years, using data from longitudinal studies, we have concluded that people do not decline significantly in most abilities, but that different generations perform at different levels of ability and with different skills. Only in the events of failing health or extremely advanced age is there noticeable and meaningful change.

Because of the difficulty of doing longitudinal studies, extremely few such research projects are found in the field of gerontology. But the few studies we have are rich with new findings that are opening up doors to new investigation and thought. While we tend to think of aging simply as biological processing, it is becoming clear that, ". . . social and psychological facts can affect biological processes at least as profoundly as biology affects behavior [Woodruff, 1975, p. 8]."

Once again, stereotypes affect our expectations, which in turn affect our future.

Before we begin a summary of the research regarding aging, test yourself on what your stereotypes are about the "natural" consequences of aging. Can you determine where your ideas came from? Consider the statements in the questionnaire shown in Table 2-1. This questionnaire is modified from one I used with medical students and other health pro-

TABLE 2-1
Myths, Stereotypes, and Realities of Aging

Statement	Factual Answer	Emotional Response
1. Most older people who live into their eighties or beyond become senile before they die.	T F	T F
2. Aged persons tend to regress and become more like they were as children.	T F	T F
3. Women are more likely to live into their later years than men.	T F	T F
4. All people start becoming more forgetful after the age of 20; older people cannot learn well.	T F	T F
5. Fewer than 10 percent of all older people are college graduates.	T F	T F
6. The majority of older people no longer have sexual desires.	T F	T F
7. As people age, they almost inevitably become more withdrawn and disengaged from life.	T F	T F
8. The majority of older people are in poor health by the age of 60.	T F	T F
9. The suicide rate is higher for the elderly than for any other age group.	T F	T F
10. As people become older, they tend to become more suspicious, complaining, and irritable.	T F	T F
11. Older people worry much more and are much more afraid than younger people; they are more cautious.	T F	T F
12. Older people can no longer produce on a job or be very active socially.	T F	T F
13. Senile behavior is always caused by brain damage.	T F	T F
14. Alcoholic beverages are more hazardous for the elderly than for other adult age groups.	T F	T F

fessionals. Try to be aware not only of the "right" answer (what your logic or information tells you is true or false), but also of what you feel (your emotional response, which may be unrelated to what you have read or what "logic" tells you). Because your logical side and your emotional side are not always in agreement, two separate columns are provided for your answers.

Although our stereotypical responses may urge us to answer true to all these statements, only statements 3, 5, and 9 are true. All of the others are false. Recent work with older people indicates that none of the assumptions in the questionnaire is organic to the aging process.

What, then, are the connections between human aging and intelligence, I.Q., the ability to learn, and senility? What is the effect of sensory changes upon intelligence and personality? And what is recent research saying about the effects of aging on such personality characteristics as cautiousness, rigidity, fear, anxiety, and happiness?

CHANGES IN INTELLIGENCE AND ABILITY

Some old people boast, "I'm just as good as I ever was." And they are!

Examples abound of people who were outstandingly creative and intellectually sharp in old age. Albert Schweitzer continued his work as a physician and philosopher until the age of 90. Justice Holmes, up to the age of 92, made distinctive contributions to the Supreme Court. Thomas Edison was experimenting and inventing in his nineties. Golda Meir was known to work productively up to twenty hours a day in her late seventies. Archibald MacLeish, at the age of 80 said, "Yeats became a great poet when he was close to sixty, and his greatest work was done later . . . I am just senile enough to be persuaded that I am likewise [to Yeats]." Bertrand Russell, English philosopher and defender of individual liberty, lived to be 98; at 78 he was awarded the Nobel Prize for Literature. Pablo Picasso, founder of the cubistic art movement, said, at the age of 86, "It takes a long time to become young." Casey Stengel was still managing winning baseball teams at an age when most men were on social security. Giuseppe Verdi was still composing operas at 80. George Bernard Shaw was writing plays at the age of 93. Albert Einstein, Amos Alonzo Stagg, Norman Thomas, Robert Frost, Karl Menninger, and George Burns all had a productive old age. Arthur Rubinstein, at the age of 80, was told that he was playing the piano better than ever. He replied:

> Now I take chances I never took before. You see, the stakes are not so high. I can afford it. I used to be so much more careful. No wrong notes. Not too bold ideas . . . . Now I let go and enjoy myself and to hell with everything except the music![1]

Pearl Buck, author and winner of the Nobel Prize, said about her life, "I have learned so much since I was seventy! I believe I can honestly say that I have learned more in the last ten years than I learned in any previous decade."[2]

Are these extraordinary people, out of our creative range? Certainly they are exceptional. However, even among the more typical older people you know, haven't you observed differences in intellectual functioning? Some seem to retain and even increase their "sharpness," while others appear to deteriorate.

The deterioration and ultimate loss of mental prowess is one of the most feared aspects of aging. Perhaps because of their own personal fears, as well as their professional interests, scientists in gerontology have done more research on the topic of human intelligence and its possible changes with aging than any other area (Botwinick, 1973, p. 181). In addition to being of great personal interest to researchers, intelligence is relatively easy to measure and thereby lends itself to easy study.

One of the most significant alterations in approach is, as we have seen, the break from cross-sectional studies. This approach ignored generational differences of education, values, and experiences, leading to untrue and unfair conclusions. When researchers found that older persons tested lower than younger persons, they concluded that intelligence declines with age. For example, Corsini and Fassett reported in 1953:

[1] Morton Puner, *To the Good Long Life: What We Know about Growing Old* (New York: Universe, 1974), p. 273.
[2] Ibid.

It is generally accepted that intelligence develops at a fairly steady rate from birth to about fifteen . . . at about twenty to twenty-five the absolute maximum of intellectual development appears to be reached . . . intelligence [then] begins a slow but steady decline.
                                                              [p. 249]

The fact that measured intelligence in the population is increasing with each decade (Botwinick, 1973, p. 193) makes cross-sectional research even less trustworthy. This increase in measured intelligence probably has to do with the longer education given people today, although early nutrition and health practices may also be involved. Most older people not only received less formal education, but their type of education relied heavily on principles of memorization rather than on methods of problem-solving.

Furthermore, intelligence tests are aged-biased. The concept of intelligence, therefore, and the instruments used to measure it are defined in terms of abilities that are important during youth and early adulthood (Baltes and Schaie, 1974, p. 37). Intelligence tests came into existence for the sole reason of predicting school performance. In addition, the tests are frequently formulated by college graduates who are usually young, middle-class, and white. They draw upon a bank of knowledge and a system of values from a language background alien to many older persons. Intelligence tests often fail as a measure of ability or intelligence when a person is not fluent in English and familiar with the culture of this country.

Also, an older person's performance can be affected by anxiety and the unfamiliarity of the test situation. Anyone can forget how to take examinations. (As every college student knows, test-taking is a special skill.) Manual dexterity, speed, eyesight, and the familiarity of instructions can all influence how well an older person does on an I.Q. test.

The change in our understanding of intelligence and of human development occurred because of a number of longitudinal studies. In a review of the relevant literature, Professor Schaie (1975) of the University of Southern California concluded that, ". . . in the areas of intellectual abilities and skills, old people, in general, if they are reasonably healthy, have not declined, but rather have become obsolete [p. 120]." Quickly, before he could be misinterpreted, Dr. Schaie adds that obsolescence can be remedied through education, that it is not inevitable, and that people who remain alert—aware of the environment and of others, sensitive to their own continued need for personal growth—will not gather the dust of becoming obsolete.

Therefore, research now points to one fact: Intellectual decline because of old age is not normal, but is largely a myth (Baltes, 1974, p. 35). For persons who are fairly healthy, such a decline is something they *permit* to happen by permitting themselves to become out-dated, by turning away from the outside world, and by keeping completely unto themselves.

When mental decline does occur, it usually results from health problems and often comes shortly before death. A University of Michigan longitudinal study found that when measures of a person's cognitive ability, such as the I.Q. test, dropped significantly, that person was more likely to die soon. Follow-up studies have confirmed this. Such sudden deterioration of intellectual functioning has been called the *terminal drop* in intelligence (Riegel & Riegel, 1972).

In addition to the terminal drop, significantly high blood pressure and other cardiovascular problems form the other major cause of decreased intelligence (Eisdorfer, 1975, p. 14). People with high blood pressure show more intellectual deficits than others who are just as old; on the other hand, those who grow old without a significant rise in blood pressure may escape entirely the intellectual decline traditionally associated with advanced age. Recent research by Wilkie and Eisdorfer (1971, p. 962) concludes that the intellectual decline customarily associated with aging may be due rather to cardiovascular illness, and not connected with the aging process at all. Obviously, good health care is crucial for full intellectual functioning. Apparently, only people who are reasonably healthy can hope to enjoy full intellectual capabilities.

Given reasonably good health and undiminished intelligence, what can we say about our ability to learn? Well, basically the old adage that "You can't teach an old dog new tricks" is true neither of dogs nor of human beings! ˎ

To be fair, some current research shows that learning declines do occur. Older adults certainly have poorer memories than younger adults, very likely the result of reduced blood circulation, and consequently less oxygen flow, to the brain (Craik, 1977). Many people have made the observation that forgetting increases with age after middle adulthood.

Though all scientists agree that older people can learn, they debate questions of speed and retention: How does aging affect older people's speed and retention? How important are the losses? On an individual basis, does a decline in speed or retention matter? For example, that younger persons can memorize forty items in a specific time, whereas older persons can remember only thirty-six, may be statistically significant. However, statistics deal only with the averages. That this difference will matter in actual life is unlikely. Further, many older persons have better learning ability than the typical younger person.

Although, on the whole, older people learn more slowly than they did when they were younger, they find ways to compensate for this. As a college instructor, I have observed that older students, who bring a greater depth of experience into the classroom situation, perform at least as well as their younger classmates. Life experience is an advantage. Then too, studies bear out that "old people compensate for loss of speed by stressing accuracy [Blum, Jarvik & Clark, 1970, p. 174]."

SENILITY AND BRAIN DAMAGE

The emotionally laden term "senility" refers to a type of chronic organic brain disorder usually considered irreversible.

Once it occurs, supposedly full recovery is impossible. The usual symptoms of senility are poor memory, impairments in time and place orientation, and a general, marked decline in intellectual functioning.

Though our examples have shown that some older persons have significant increases in their intellectual abilities and that learning can continue throughout life, the myth that if a person lives long enough, senility is inevitable, is still cherished and popular. And as long as most people cling to the myth, the myth will produce self-fulfilling results.

Picture the following experiment. Imagine it as *vividly* as you can:

Three college-age students are told that they will discuss an important topic and that their talk will be tape-recorded. However, two of the students are instructed to treat the third student as if she/he were old. The third student does not know about the secret instructions. The two "young" students then hold a discussion, but exclude, ignore, and even subtly belittle the "old" student. In a series of these experiments, the excluded student manifested a range of emotional reactions, but in every case the "old" student began to ramble, to become inattentive, or to make inappropriate comments.

Dr. Tom Leo Smith (1975), a social psychologist from the University of Denver, conducted this experiment many times with a number of students over a nine-month period. He then had judges listen to tape-recordings of the discussions and analyze what happened. The judges, who never saw the speakers, concluded that the "old" students were "slightly senile" because they seemed forgetful, they reminisced about the past, and they talked about nonrelevant subjects. The judges estimated that the "old" students were at least in their mid-sixties; the youngest age estimation was 63. From his studies, Dr. Smith concluded that *producing* the symptoms of senility is possible, even in young adults, simply by having others treat them as if they were old.

Health professionals often refer to old people as "crocks," assuming senility. The assumption is harmful. Their attitude not only contributes to the condition and influences the treatment, but also, according to Dr. Smith's experiment, produces the symptoms.

Unfortunately, physicians and other professionals often attempt to measure the degree of senility by asking patients inappropriate questions—completely ignoring the possibility that the patient is simply emotionally upset or in pain. For example, a medical student and I were talking to a patient in a nursing home. The patient told us she had not seen her physician for almost a month, and she very much wished she could ask him some questions. She was in her seventies and dying of cancer. Numbed by pain medication, she was slow in her responses but completely coherent: She was discussing with us some of her feelings about death and dying. Suddenly a man came into the room and began to ask questions: "What day and month is this?" . . . "Who is President of the United States?" I watched her face change from a startled look to a blank expression. As he took her pulse, he continued to administer the senility test: "Do you know what place you're in?" She replied, "Doctor, what's happening to me?" Obviously taking her question as an indication of lack of orientation, he said, as he left the room, "You're in a hospital being taken care of." When the doctor was gone, she began to cry from frustration; and, as her crying signaled emotional instability, the nurse came in and gave her a sedative.

Senility is a convenient label for people with whom you do not wish to expend time or effort. It justifies hurrying by them: If they are senile, they are beyond helping. An *Esquire* magazine article ("How to Get Old and Do It Right," April, 1973) jokingly said that, "Americans hate old people because . . . they whine, intrude, make you feel guilty, pretend they're senile . . . accordingly, younger Americans retaliate by creating detention centers like nursing homes and Miami Beach to get the old out of sight [p. 73]."

What senility is, however, is still unclear. Some physicians say, "there is no such thing [Townsend, 1971, p. 125]." Senility is a word much over-used, little understood, and possibly devoid of medical meaning.

Often it is simply a label put on an older person who has a mental illness. Older people do suffer the kinds of brain change that results in behavior which we have called "senile." Mental illness in the elderly certainly exists, but it is often unrelated to brain damage and aging. Yet a young person who acts disoriented is treated for mental illness; an old person displaying similar symptoms is called senile and given custodial care.

In a tour of a nursing home, some students and I were taken through the "back wards." They were dimly lit and smelled of urine. Old women sat lined up in chairs along one side of the hallway, a television set facing them. None of them talked to each other; most of them sat either staring into space or dozingly slumped in chairs. As we walked past these women, the nurse turned back to the students and said, "As you can see, this is where we keep our senile patients." One of the old women looked up, her face showing comprehension. Tears rolled down her cheeks and she shook her head. "No . . . ," she said, " . . . oh God, is it true?" Patients who enter nursing homes to recuperate from an illness and hospitalization that have left them temporarily confused are likely to remain confused because of their isolation and the way they are treated.

Distinguishing functional mental illness from irreversible brain damage is often difficult. Older persons who show no brain disease sometimes behave as if they had serious mental impairment, ". . . while others with profound brain damage have only mild disorders. Even normal elderly individuals can have brain changes which appear as marked as those in individuals with clinically obvious senile or arteriosclerotic disorder [Butler & Lewis, 1973, p. 75]."

If aging is not the cause of what we call senility, what is? The causes of brain damage, both reversible and irreversible, include infection, congestive heart failure, drugs, accidents, alcohol, liver failure, dehydration, cerebrovascular accidents (such as stroke), and brain tumor.

Only recently, scientists discovered that senility also can result from chronic malnutrition (Hoffer, 1972, p. 45). In 1940 the Japanese put two thousand captured Canadian soldiers into prisoner-of-war camps for almost four years, where they suffered chronic malnutrition. Twenty-five years later, when the men were middle-aged, they showed signs of senility and extreme aging. A dozen exception cases involved men who had taken massive quantities of vitamins for a long period of time after their release to make up for the deficiencies they had suffered. They were normal and healthy. Hoffer concluded that ". . . when people are long deprived of nutritional supplements, especially vitamins, they may acquire . . . senility [p. 46]."

A fascinating recent study posed the question, "Can brain damage be overcome?" Brain tissue was removed from animals of various ages. The animals were then exposed to either enriched or impoverished environments. Those animals who were given enriched experiences improved in their functioning and were able to solve standard problems. Tests done on the animals showed brain tissue growth, regardless of the age of the animals. By contrast, the animals living in impoverished environments showed all the signs of brain damage, did not improve, and showed no signs of brain tissue growth (*Science News*, 1975b). A similar experiment further disclosed that enriching experiences that brought growth and recovery only needed to happen for part of the day. Two hours a day of a stimulating environment was just as beneficial as twenty-four hours (Rosenzweig and Bennett, 1976). This discovery has fascinating implications for the rehabilitation of hospitalized older people.

A young physician (Beernink, 1970) wrote a poem about one of his patients in a similar situation:

"P. Fulton Dimmit"
Senility

They brought him from the farm in West County
When his soiling the bed every day

Made too much linen for the old washing machine
Now that his daughter's new baby arrived.

Searching for new conversation
When he'd been several weeks on my ward
I remarked on the pot of fresh rose buds
That always guarded his wrinkled form.

For an instant he seemed to grow younger
As a memory swelled in his throat,
"In my garden I'd let them die right on the plant,
It's so much better for the roots."[3]

The most prevalent stereotypes and myths about aging refer to intellectual functioning. Though knowledge and awareness can increase throughout life, learning can continue at any age, and senility is often a misdiagnosis, another aspect of aging is also heavily cloaked in stereotypes and myths: changes in personality.

PERSONALITY CHANGES AND AGING

"Older people are conservative. They are cautious. They have rigid personalities. They resist change. Older people constrict their living. They become asocial. They are self-centered, selfish, and egocentric. They worry a great deal and have many fears. They change into people different from whom they were when they were younger."

Have you heard or thought similar things? Could you add to this list? Take a moment and imagine your own personality when you are older. Will you be conservative? Rigid? Cautious? Have you wondered if these changes are already happening to you?

None of these personality changes are inevitable. However, an individual can become confused by the stereotypes. I recall

[3] From *Ward Rounds*, 2nd ed., by K. Dale Beernink (Wallingford, Penn.: Washington Square East, 1970), p. 35.

an extreme example of this in one of my clients. Mrs. B was a widow in her mid-forties, a teacher who lived in Berkeley, California. Though she sought psychotherapy because of "family problems," part of her problem was her defensive attitude about her age.

Mrs. B knew that one of the popular stereotypes about older people was that they were supposed to be more conservative. The popular saying among young liberals at that time was, "Never trust anyone over the age of thirty." My client worried about when the change was going to happen to her. A number of times she wondered if it had already happened, and she was not aware of it. She was a proud woman who saw herself as progressive and liberal; she was also lonely, a widow for several years. Because her teenage children were an important part of her life, she felt threatened by the possibility of their alienation, especially on the basis of her age.

Meanwhile, Mrs. B's house had been turned into a commune by her teenage children and was becoming an informal headquarters for the Sexual Freedom League. She felt extremely unhappy and uncomfortable with what was happening; it strained the traditional values of her upbringing. But, she was unable to say "no" to her children. She was afraid of alienating them, and she also doubted her motives. Wasn't this a sign of aging? Didn't this prove that she was not able to "keep up with the times"?

In my experience, older people are inclined to acquiesce, rather than remain true to their values, to avoid being labeled as rigid and dogmatic. They tend to be too eager to please others. Acquiescence, however, is not related to aging but rather to factors in the social environment.

Mrs. B had succumbed to the "Detroit Syndrome": Only the latest model of life values and lifestyles was alluring. Eventually, with the help of counseling, she got back in touch with herself and her own values. She changed her living situation. Somewhat to her surprise, her children accepted the changes, because they respected her "centering" as an individual.

In a complicated, reverse way, the stereotypes about aging manipulated Mrs. B. In behaving anti-stereotypically—not being rigid, conventional, and so on—she lost herself and became acquiescent to her children.

Mrs. B typifies, in an exaggerated way, the confusion many people experience on this point. Many "old-age" traits actually have nothing to do with age. Cautiousness and conservatism are examples. In my clinical observation, people admittedly tend to become more conservative, cautious, and constricted as they grow older. These changes are almost always related to insecurity, because in our society as most people age they have fewer options—both personally and financially. And the natural reaction to shrinking opportunity is to hold on to what you have.

> *Security is a glass wall*
> *full security is a glass case*
> *that keeps out all happiness,*
> *pain, awareness, change, love,*
> *danger, truth*
>   *and air*[4]

"The aged person tends to see the world as complex and perhaps even dangerous, and he responds by being more mild or conforming [Boyd & Oakes, 1969, p. 124]." Many people, even at a young age, seek out security. This striving "for the future" affects a person's lifestyle and values, and influences personality.

Even when insecurity is not an issue, generational differences in values create an illusion of personality changes due to aging. For example, marijuana was not common when older people of today were growing up; today, through widespread use, it is part of our culture. Young people feel that older people who do not accept their use of marijuana are rigid and conservative. However, these older people are being nothing

[4] Paul Williams, *Das Energi* (New York: Electra Books, 1973), p. 120.

more than consistent. Sometimes the core values and attitudes we grow up with change as we grow older, but more often they do not. Most older people have not changed what they think about marijuana or "free sex." But the times we live in have changed.

These changing times thus reduce the validity of much of our research. Because our studies on rigidity and conservatism are cross-sectional (Botwinick, 1973, p. 89), they are comparisons not only between people of different ages but also between the values of different eras. Both research and our own observations of attitudes on contemporary issues indicate that there are distinct value differences from generation to generation (Fengler and Ward, 1972, p. 124). We must realize that because of the prestige assigned to youth and novelty in our culture, we have a tendency to invalidate as old-fashioned the values of yesterday.

That old people are resistant to change is a myth (Butler & Lewis, 1973, p. 22); but that most people cling to their basic ethical values is true. When conservatism does occur, it is often due to social or economic pressures or to increased vulnerability due to health or sensorimotor problems. Greater caution in decision making can arise from basic insecurity and lack of self-confidence.

Given all the variables related to educational background, experience, social class, and profession, any comparison of personality changes must be tenuous. A study by Louis Bachtold and Emmy Werner (1971), however, was unique in that it cross-sectionally compared personality traits of three generations of women with similar educational, professional, and social background. At the University of California, Bachtold and Werner compared the personality profiles of 375 women psychologists representing three decades, with mean ages of 65, 50, and 38. All these women were teaching in academic settings, and came from similar educational backgrounds. The findings indicated that ". . . academic women of three different generations who have pursued psychology as their profession resemble each other [p. 278]." They were found to be much more like one another than like women of any age in the general population, especially in their greater drive, flexibility, nonconformity, and independence. Other studies substantiate that, ". . . the evidence to date is that older people are no more rigid or conforming than younger people [Bennett & Eckman, 1973, p. 592]." This conclusion contradicts other studies that discover major differences between generations! Similar education and living environments seem to lead to considerably fewer personality differences between young and old.

The phrase "more conservative" is usually meant to be a negative commentary on a person. And it need not be. In many ways, older people become more conservative out of the wisdom of experience! They know what the realities of life are. The flamboyant excesses of youth lose their appeal as the older person learns to conserve. Conservatism can also be a positive and necessary way of relating to life. Since the elderly often have less energy, less money, less physical strength, and less time, they need to conserve what they have, to use what they have more wisely.

One of the most impressive studies on personality and aging was recently published by Maas and Kuypers (1975), a forty-year longitudinal study of 142 relatively affluent Californians born at the turn of the century. Among the major findings of the study was that, "Popular beliefs that aging ushers in a massive decline in psychological functioning or a narrowing down of ways to live find no support in our evidence [p. 200]." In fact, personality continuities and constancies were "the most remarkable of our findings." People were shown to have lifestyles and personalities in old age similar to those they had in young adulthood.

> Old age merely continues what earlier years have launched. Finally, even when young adulthood is too narrowly lived or painfully overburdened, the later years may offer new opportunities. Different ways of living may be developed as our social environments change

with time—and as we change them. In this study we have found repeated evidence that *old age can provide a second and better chance at life.*   *[p. 215, italics ours]*

Growth is possible at any age.

Other studies indicate that most older people seldom experience major personality change with age, except as a result of specific situations for specific individuals (Neugarten, 1977). Growing older does not transform you into a different creature; there is a continuity in personality development throughout life (Mischel, 1969, p. 1,012). Aging does not separate who you are from who you will become. Certainly, we may continue to evolve, but the changes may provide "a second and better chance at life." Hence, "the joy of aging."

To live is to grow. Aging does not destroy the continuity of who we are, who we have been, or what we will become. However, like any other art, successful aging requires preparation. The first step is to free ourselves from stereotypic thinking and conditioned fears.

If we do not know what we are going to be, we cannot know what we are: let us recognize ourselves in this old man or in that old woman. It must be done if we are to take upon ourselves the entirety of our human state.   *[Simone de Beauvoir, 1973, p. 14]*

We are fortunate. Most of us have more education than our elders. We can choose our style of living from a range of options; we have many choices of how to live and grow as individuals. In the next chapter we will explore some of these options. We will discuss some of the ways to enrich our lives, starting now, which will lead to the pleasures of aging.

Three

AGING: A TIME FOR OPENING TO NEW EXPERIENCES

I was hiking alone in the Sierra Nevada mountains, intending to meet some friends at a camp about ten miles from the nearest road. It was a sunny August afternoon, but at ten thousand feet the weather was brisk. I rushed along the trail, enjoying the walk but eager to arrive at camp. This was an isolated part of the Sierras; there was no one else on the trail.

About half-way there, I was startled at a strange sight on the trail ahead of me. A woman was hiking alone, just as I was —but she was elderly, probably about 75. She was short, slender, with white hair. I stopped to watch her with fascination and enjoyment. She wore a backpack and white gloves, and she walked slowly, using a cane. I watched as she stopped to look at things along the trail, obviously engrossed, and in no hurry.

To see an old person hiking alone, deep in the Sierras,

was incredible! In twenty years of mountaineering, I had never seen anyone backpacking who was much past the age of 60.

I caught up with the woman, and we hiked together. I asked her to tell me about herself. She said she was glad for my companionship, but she preferred to walk together and enjoy the sights around us. She did not feel like talking about herself, but perhaps later. Walking with her, I found myself thoroughly enjoying her special enthusiasm and curiosity.

We came to a lovely stream banked by white granite rocks and bordered by pine trees and wildflowers. My companion said she wanted to camp here for the night—her first night of sleeping outside in the mountains. "This is exactly what I had pictured!" she said. When I asked if she backpacked often, she replied that this was her introductory trip to the mountains.

She went on to explain that she lived in San Francisco and had grown up there; she said she was born "before the turn of the century." Recently, she had been reading books by John Muir, the naturalist, who had hiked the mountains and wrote of the beauty of nature. She had also heard of "young people" who enjoyed hiking and camping in the mountains, and she was curious to find out what it was like for herself. None of her friends hiked or went camping, and she was not able to interest them in trying something new and coming along with her. She went to a mountaineering store and asked to rent a sleeping bag and "everything else you need to camp in the mountains." She commented that the shop people were wonderfully helpful. "Several of the young employees offered to take me with them when they went next time," she said. However, she decided she preferred to go alone because "it's more of an adventure that way. I slept several nights on an air mattress in my backyard in San Francisco . . . to make sure that my old bones could take it. I did fine, so here I am!"

I never learned her name or anything more about her.

Several days later I met an old friend who was a ranger and naturalist for Yosemite National Park. Almost his first words to me were, "I met the most remarkable woman yesterday!"

He went on to tell me that he had led a hike up Lambert Dome, one of Yosemite's mountains. The mountain sits twelve thousand feet high in the middle of a beautiful alpine meadow and presents a climb of two thousand feet that takes all day. The park rangers offer free guided mountain climbs that are previously announced; those who wish to go simply show up at the scheduled time and place. On that particular day, at eight o'clock in the morning, an old woman came to the meeting place. She was elderly, white-haired, slender, wearing a backpack, and carrying a cane—my hiking companion!

The ranger said he was worried about her participation. Would she be all right? Could she keep up with the others? He told her that the hike would be strenuous. She said, "Fine, I hope I won't be too slow . . . if I am, I'll take care of myself, and you go on ahead." What could the ranger say? He wished she would stay behind, but did not know what else to say to discourage her. So, the group set out.

The woman walked slowly, the ranger said, but she did manage to keep up or at least within sight of the group. Finally, they all reached the top of the mountain. People sat and enjoyed the view. The old woman, who was the last to reach the top, sat down and rested. Then she reached into her backpack and pulled out a bottle of champagne! "This is the first mountain I've ever climbed," she said. "Would anyone like to help me celebrate?"

Prior to meeting the elderly woman on the mountain, I had thought of older people in terms of the standard stereotypes. I found it difficult to identify with any of them; they were almost like a different species of human being. This one woman, in her extraordinary openness to new experiences, changed my whole perspective on life and aging.

That people can continue to grow now seems obvious to me. They can continue to live excitingly, to develop potentials *at any age*. But until I met this woman, I assumed that old age was all grief and no joy—and I dreaded it.

In recent years, psychologists have searched for a *positive* theory of human development—one that includes the latter half of life. The human potential and growth movement grew out of one such positive approach called *humanistic psychology.*

What is our growth potential as we age? What does "maturity" mean? What are the qualities of a self-actualizing person, and how can we continue to grow throughout life? In exploring how to stay young and fully alive—developing, thriving, and expanding—we will look at two dimensions of self-development: (1) growing with other people and (2) greater awareness of one's self and one's past.

THEORIES OF HUMAN DEVELOPMENT

In the study of child development, the direction of change is clear: The child is meant to grow in size and maturity. However, growth potential in adulthood is ambiguous: change may be positive or negative. Are adults even meant to grow? If so, in what direction? What is the meaning of stability, decline, growth, or environmental determinism?

Four conflicting concepts of aging have emerged from the social and natural sciences over the years. The first three are included here for purposes of comparison; the fourth is the thesis of this chapter.

1. *Adult development is one of decline.* What grows and ripens must eventually decay and decline. The concept is borrowed from the natural sciences and is based on a biological analogy.
2. *Adult development is one of stability.* Adults tend to stabilize after adolescence. Change occurs primarily through trauma or accident. This concept is based primarily on psychoanalytical thought. The subtle implication is that change is negative. Freud thought that identity is established by the end of childhood and produces fairly consistent behavior thereafter, modified largely by trauma or accident.
3. *Adult development is one of response to a cultural or environmental stimulus.* Change is determined by an individual's ability to respond to his/her surroundings with few personality predis-

positions. Personality is shaped by, and is the sum of, the environment, including social experiences and roles. This concept also implies negativism in that the individual is molded by the environment, or by others, and is not in reality one "individual." This perspective has been fostered, in part, by the various schools of sociology and behavior modification.

4. *Adult development is one of continued growth.* Adults have the ability to be self-actualizing throughout life. Any age contains a potential for "maturity" (Vispo), "becoming" (Allport), development of the "creative self" and the striving for superiority (Adler), a growing "concept of self" (Jung), of "self-actualization" (Maslow, Rogers). Our natural development is toward growth; life is a process of expansion. This concept, more than any of the others, looks upon change as potentially positive.

In all honesty, all four theories are supported by the lives of people I know. There are those who decline with aging; those who seem unchanged; those who are products of their environments; and those who continue to grow. The fact is, nothing about human development is automatic or inevitable.

I know from clinical experience that many people in this country are so caught up in their daily lives (reacting to the pressures of the moment, making ends meet, and other problems) that they never stop to consider what they will be like in ten, twenty, or forty years. This lack of forethought (not to mention preparation) for their extended futures is one explanation for the bitterness and frustration many older people seem to feel. Somehow, life has *happened to them,* and they are unhappy with it. They never looked up from their daily existence to see the choices in life. The elderly woman hiking alone in the Sierras excited my sense of life. I was moved by her openness to new experiences, by her capacity for living in the present, and by her sense of adventure.

Now, while the future is still within the reach of your imagination, is the perfect time to recognize the choices: How will I like to grow older? What am I going to choose for *my* maturing and *my* life? And you can still choose, no matter how old you now are.

My basic assumption is that we have the freedom to choose who we are becoming, if we are willing to clarify what we would like for ourselves as we grow older. Life can either happen *to* us or we can become conscious agents in creating our own lives.

In seeking our truth, we expand on that of others and combine relevant features with our own. Which goal fits the unique person you are? What style of living do you choose and wish to become responsible for? Is increased introversion something you see happening to you? Then how much turning inward do you choose to allow? And what other qualities and values, in what combination, do you claim for yourself?

Humanistic psychology, a recent movement sometimes referred to as a "third force" along with psychoanalysis and behaviorism, provides an orientation in which individuals can determine their own lives and take responsibility for what they become. A basic tenet of psychoanalysis is that people are guided through life by instinctive drives.

Humanistic psychology sets off in a direction away from both psychoanalysis and behaviorism. For example, Freud, the originator of psychoanalysis, stated that people rigidify as they grow older, that old people are no longer educable (Butler, 1967, p. 43). Yet, as Kastenbaum (1965) states, "Old age is one of the few topics that Freud did not illuminate with fresh observations and insights [p. 26]." Behaviorism, another important school of psychology, approaches aging as "the psychology of adapting to losses [Preston, 1973, p. 64]." Both Freudianism and behaviorism emphasize our continuity with the animal and mechanistic world.

Humanistic psychology, on the other hand, relates to those characteristics and capacities that make people uniquely *different from* the lower animals. It focuses on the whole person and on "the worth, dignity, rights, responsibilities, and fulfillment" of people (Sutich & Vich, 1969, p. 8). The humanistic emphasis is on the growth and development of potential. Self-fulfillment and self-actualization are the main themes in life; psychotherapy, if needed, removes the barriers to personal growth.

Some of the essential concepts of humanistic psychology are summarized by Stein (1973, p. 7) as follows:

1. People are inherently good (as opposed to some theories that conceive of people as basically evil).
2. People have psychological needs for security, love, belonging, creativity, and self-actualization that are as innate as our physiological needs.
3. Our understanding of ourselves can only come by studying human beings, not animals.
4. Although we are certainly influenced by our past experiences and our environment, we have the power to make decisions and to be responsible for our choices.

Comparatively little is known about the psychology of healthy adult growth, development, and maturity. We have long studied child development and, more recently, the changes that happen to old people, especially in nursing homes. But we know little about what happens to healthy people between adolescence and old age.

THEORIES OF LIFE CYCLE, MATURITY, AND AGING

In gerontology, most of the ideas on human development focus on adaptation. Basically two contrasting theories (Havighurst, 1961, p. 8) deal with successful aging:

1. The *disengagement theory* states that people withdraw from society as they age, while at the same time society withdraws from them. According to this theory, disengagement is to be expected and is actually adaptive. At about age 50, the individual, desiring a disengagement from active life, begins to establish a new process of diminishing involvement.

2. The *activity theory* espouses the American formula for happiness: "Keep busy." Successful aging means maintaining all your activities and involvements in society. By middle-age, people have reached the level of achievement and outward-directed lifestyle that is comfortable for them as individuals. This level should be maintained indefinitely for happiness and fulfillment.

Though these polarized lifestyles are applicable and satisfactory for some people, research has rejected both disengagement and activity theory as universal, inevitable processes (Tissue, 1971, p. 76). More often, we find an integration of or a shifting between both.

Evidence and/or authorities can be found to support either theory.

Consistent with disengagement theory, gerontologist Bernice Neugarten takes a developmental view similar to that of Carl Jung, who theorized that people become more introverted as they grow older. Studies conducted by the Human Development Committee at the University of Chicago indicate that often "people become more preoccupied with the inner life" as they age (Neugarten, 1972, p. 10). Activities are then likely to change from community involvement to more solitary pursuits, such as reading or gardening. Neugarten describes this process as *"increased interiority . . .* [where people] attend increasingly to the control and satisfaction of personal needs [p. 10]."

In favor of the activity theory, a longitudinal research project by Palmore (1973) followed 127 people over a ten-year period. When the study began, the average age of the subjects was 68. During this ten-year period, with measurements taken every few years, there were "almost no overall reductions in either activities or [changes in] attitudes [toward activities, p. 260]." These findings contradict the common opinion that most people grow less active as they age; it also suggests that although people may reduce certain activities, they frequently compensate by increasing their involvement in other areas of living.

Most theories of human development, in fact, imply stages of growth, such as "integration" (Erickson); "increased interiority" (Neugarten); or "contemplation" (Vispo). Human growth may be seen as a hierarchy—steps on a ladder that one climbs toward the final attainment—or as a continuing process of becoming. The latter view, as espoused by Rogers and Maslow, assumes that all persons have an innate force for growth and that self-fulfillment is the main theme in human life. A person has inner capabilities and potentialities; human development is growth toward realizing or actualizing that which is within. We all strive toward self-actualization.

Abraham Maslow studied people who, in his opinion, had realized their potentialities to the fullest; he wanted to define the characteristics of healthy people. The following is a composite description of those people:

1. Self-actualizing persons are *realistic* in orientation.
2. They *accept* themselves and others and the natural world for what these are.
3. They have a great deal of *spontaneity* and openness to new experiences.
4. They are *problem-centered.*
5. They have a desire for *privacy* and often have an air of detachment.
6. They are autonomous and *independent* in making up their own minds.
7. They have a *freshness of appreciation* and a richness of emotional reactions.
8. They have a high frequency of *peak experiences.*
9. They *identify* with the human species.
10. They have *relationships* with others which tend to be *deep* and *profound*, rather than superficial or shallow.
11. Their values and attitudes are *democratic.*
12. They are *creative*, though not necessarily "productive" in the usual sense of being artists. They are original, ingenious, and inventive in living.
13. They resist simple conformity to the culture and instead have their own *value system.* They are free from many of our social pressures.

Maslow (1962) insisted that human development is a process and "not the stepwise, all or none, conception of progression [p. 19]."

No one final process of growth applies to everyone. Becoming philosophical or introverted, staying active, increasing your creativity, growing in spontaneity, developing deeper relationships with others—any or all of these may be part of your growth. And allowing for change is, of course, part of the process. Developing and utilizing yourself is the full orchestration of your personal symphony; the directions in which you grow are your private melody.

The sum of self-actualization is creating a style of living for yourself that allows for continuing growth and health.

Medicine, in attempting to define "health," has recently realized that healthy people can throw light on the diseased. Health maintenance is becoming increasingly important in medicine: Illness can be prevented by learning more about how people stay healthy and then by applying this knowledge. Likewise, in psychology, the question "What keeps people healthy?" is just as important as "What makes people sick?"

Does it matter which side of the coin we study? Is the glass half full or half empty? Most health professionals spend their careers studying people who are sick. To study disease without inquiring into health is to work with a partial, distorted perspective. Disease represents only one side of the coin, only the empty half of the glass, and only a part of the person.

Maslow states that if psychologists study the crippled, stunted, and neurotic, they are bound to produce a crippled psychology. In both medicine and psychology, health professionals can describe sickness more easily because, traditionally, we have spent most of our time attempting to cure patients. But now we are turning our attention to aiding the healthy to become more functional, the contented more fulfilled, and the normal person more self-actualized.

One of my students gave a succinct definition of health: "Health means feeling good." We are exploring ways to teach people how to keep themselves "feeling good."

NEW EXPERIENCES WITH SELF AND OTHERS: GROWTH GROUPS FOR OLDER PEOPLE

This revised emphasis by health professionals has circulated among the general public. Growth groups, sensitivity groups, T-groups, or encounter groups have sprung up all over. For example, a man phoned my office asking for a recommendation to a growth group, because he wanted to "keep growing as a person." We met for an hour so I could explore with him what kind of growth experience he wanted. I learned that Mr. R was 55, happily married, a high school dropout, and a plumber. He felt content with most of his life, able to cope with the problems of earning a living and raising four children, but he felt a "general restlessness . . . a boredom . . . because I'm stagnating." Mr. R had heard about growth groups from his sister-in-law, who had had a good experience in one. As we talked, Mr. R's basic interests became clear: (1) exploring himself with other people in a group and (2) adventuring into himself—opening the doors of his unique life history—by starting a personal journal.

Mr. R sought greater happiness by becoming more conscious of his growth. He saw, as Lowen (1975) did, that "Happiness is the consciousness of growth [p. 33]." Growth groups can help overcome some of the alienation of modern life. Sidney Jourard, author of *The Transparent Self* (1971), states that people have a need to make themselves known to others; self-disclosure and sharing add to self-knowledge and are part of living a healthy life. The majority of those who attend growth groups are under the age of thirty. But a handful of psychotherapists, aware that not only the young feel alienated in modern, mass society, are forming growth groups for older people.

In fact, a person's need for interaction may actually increase with age. Robert Marcus (1974), who has led growth groups for hundreds of retired people (ages 62 to 97), has found that older people quickly open up to experiences of love, warmth, and intimacy. Supported by the group, they are able to look at issues such as death with a surprising frankness and freedom. His group sessions are often centered around a theme (less sensitive leaders might dismiss them as being "too intellectual") such as grandchildren, nutrition, finances, death, and leisure time, all topics of real concern to older people.

Dr. Marcus writes about what happens in a group: Mrs. C begins by expressing her unhappiness with her grandchildren and children. "They never phone . . . they never write . . . they forget about me unless they need something." But when she hears other group members talk about becoming less involved with children ("I spend money on myself now, as well as my grandchildren . . ."), Mrs. C begins to relax and becomes less desperate, because others share her plight. She is not a failure as a parent. Or if she is, she has lots of company among people she values! After several group sessions Mrs. C becomes more self-giving, focusing less on her expectations and disappointments with her children. She writes and phones them less; as the group has replaced some of her frustrated needs she clings less to her family, which improves her relationship with them dramatically. Feeling less obliged, the family members are able to become more giving.

One of the saddest things that happens to older people in our society is that they become *isolated by dishonesty.* In this way, groups can also serve an extremely important function.

A tone of artificiality sometimes characterizes people's relations with the elderly. Many people have negative feelings toward the older person, and, ashamed of these feelings, they often assume a false pose of respect and interest. How many times have you seen someone talking to an older person and, though outwardly respectful and interested, he or she is obviously eager to get away? A growth group is sometimes the only place where older people can experience honesty with others. Otherwise, they live in a world of bland and superficial cheerfulness, a world of isolation.

One group in particular has enabled older people to participate fully and actively, under leadership that is supportive and compassionate.

The SAGE Project

The Senior Actualization and Growth Explorations Project (SAGE) was formed by Gay Luce, a science writer and expert on mental health, in January, 1974. She was a director of the project until 1977. Gay started SAGE because of her conviction that "aging can be a creative interplay of the forces of life rather than a deterioration process." Her idea was to apply many of the techniques developed by the human potential movement and ancient disciplines to the revitalization of older people.

SAGE was originally a pilot study, involving a group of twelve people between the ages of 67 and 77. The original group met weekly for discussing and sharing, as well as for experiments in massage, deep breathing, relaxation training, yoga, awareness exercises, meditation, body movement, biofeedback relaxation, exploration of private fantasies and dreams, and group art experiences.

Word spread quickly, and the project has been swamped with requests to take on more people and extend services. Health professionals from throughout the United States have traveled for professional training with the SAGE project, using their new expertise to start groups in their own communities.[1]

[1] SAGE is now a nationally known organization with a staff of twenty-five, in addition to two hundred and fifty trainees, interns, and participants. Its program is being brought to five Bay Area institutions for the aged, nursing homes, and convalescent hospitals. A video tape documentary on SAGE, shot by Richard Fairman on a low budget, has won an award and has been viewed by over fifty thousand people. Kenneth Dychtwald has lectured extensively, presenting SAGE ideas and stimulating the formation of many similar groups around the country. Out of this work has evolved the National Association for Humanistic Gerontology. As the older participants have taken more leadership, SAGE has begun to fulfill some of its early dreams of a "grass roots" network and of setting a model for all the positive things one can expect in old age. In 1976 SAGE was awarded a three-year National Institute for Mental Health (NIMH) grant, which covers its core program. Many important activities do not fit into current grants, and SAGE is interested in funding these, too. SAGE has begun the use of video teaching tapes. A tape on fundamental breathing exercises is now available. Two documentaries can

For a young project with extremely limited funds, SAGE had a remarkable impact. Participants have told me that their experience at SAGE has been one of the most exciting, positive events in their mature lives.

I talked with Gay Luce and asked her some questions:

LIL: Gay, what are some of the general results of your SAGE groups?

GAY: We have seen a powerful affirmation that older people, given guidance and support, can experience aging as a time of culmination and flowering, a period of growth at least as exciting as childhood.

When I started the SAGE project for older people, I realized it was difficult for them to get this kind of experience. There are many growth programs for younger people, who usually can find the money and transportation; but for older people, the mechanics can be overwhelming. What we did was to offer as much of the human potential and growth movement as we could in a small, local center. Some of our older participants had gone to Esalen and other growth centers, because they were curious and interested. But they disliked being the only older person there. Moreover, usually those places were uncomfortable.

Many of the human growth techniques used with younger people have to be modified for the older person who may be physically out of shape. We are constantly experimenting and creating new exercises that work.

Older people are generally cut off from the opportunities to learn about self-care and inner growth. They sometimes lack money, mobility, and sophistication in utilizing the available resources in the community. Professional services for health care and education are generally institutional and are aimed at narrowly defined problems. There are some attempts to provide food, housing, and medical aid, yet *many older people are finding themselves trivialized and denigrated,* rather than experiencing an enhancement of consciousness and fulfillment of potential that should come after a lifetime of experience. So, the project was originally aimed to serve the needs of those older people who had few resources elsewhere.

---

be rented: "A New Image of Aging" and "Coming of Age." Dr. Gay Luce is currently writing a book on SAGE. SAGE is located in the Claremont Hotel, Berkeley, California.

LIL: I know from talking to some of your group participants that there have been many dramatic long-term results for people in your groups. Could you describe what usually happens?

GAY: People change and open up in different ways, depending on who they are and where they are starting from. For example, some of the people who came to the groups at the nursing homes appeared senile at first. However, with support and stimulation, some of them began to interact with others, to be more connected and coherent. In our core groups, we have seen people getting through some of their major life blocks. For example, shy people became much more outgoing. One woman, who had always been inhibited, found herself enjoying sexual contact with her husband for the first time in her life.

Many people have felt secure enough in SAGE groups to learn how to express emotions. This allowed them to become closer to others and to help each other. Individuals have liberated themselves from the seemingly minor yet crippling anxieties, diffidences, and fears that have burdened them for much of their lives.

Regarding health, some people have removed physical symptoms that they had for decades. For example, in learning relaxation, people usually start to sleep better and in some instances blood pressure has lowered. One woman cured herself of migraine headaches. Many people have found that they need fewer drug medications as they have learned relaxation techniques. The symptoms of arthritis have been diminished for some participants. People also report that they have much less depression. For some, memory is improved simply by less frequent use of tranquilizers and sedatives, since these medications certainly affect psychological functioning.

Most important, SAGE members have become more conscious of themselves as the major actors in their lives, with the power to make choices and take control.

LIL: I've attended a number of the group meetings and I know how enjoyable and meaningful they are to the participants. What do you think is important in a group meeting?

GAY: We want a relaxed and intimate group feeling in which people feel free to share anything. We want to support each individual and encourage people to become *un*self-conscious and *un*competitive. People show a lot of affection for each other, touching and caring, and also becoming more candid. There are also periods of being with oneself, in silence—we do guided fantasies to help people get more in touch with themselves (chanting, music, art, and meditation). We do physical exercises, body movement, and relaxation, and psychological explorations. The aim is never to perform or produce—but to experience one's own possibilities. And we talk about new ideas, such as nutrition and self-healing.

LIL: Could you describe what you consider to be a typical meeting?

GAY: There is no "usual" pattern any more . . . . People come in greeting each other, hugging, and talking. Often we have a period of structured silence and centering. This is often followed by some kind of exercise, body movement and breathing awareness. (Anything done at the physical level also has a spiritual and emotional component. Exercise is done not just to oxygenate tissues and make them limber—it's also to enable people to get into themselves and to fully experience their bodies.)

An important part of our program has been its holistic quality. We want to enrich people at *all* levels. Disciplines of mind and emotions encourage deep inner development. Many exercises that can be performed purely for physical well being, such as Tai Chi or Yoga, gain a dimension when presented thoughtfully, for then they engage the spirit and enlarge the individual's consciousness. Thus, the same relaxation that aids physical health can be the gateway to new experiences of the vastness of an individual's inner space, and provide a bridge to meditation. A breathing exercise invigorates the nervous system and at the same time can cause the breather to enjoy with reverence the life-giving energy that comes to him from the air and the sun. This introduces an expansive relatedness to the larger universe.

Often a group meeting ends with a general discussion time and evaluation of the session. The discussion may focus on thoughts that someone would like to share from the group experiences, or concerns from life outside the group, or perhaps some general ideas that are educational.

LIL: What do you consider the most important thing for older people to learn in your groups?

GAY: The cornerstone of our program and initial step is the teaching of deep relaxation by a variety of methods. This does not mean just physical relaxation: It means letting go emotionally, quieting one's mind and affirming one's trust in the rightness of the universe.

Learning how to relax has brought pronounced changes in the lives of many of our participants. For example, one man came into the program because of tension: Within two months he was no longer having headaches, no longer needed tranquilizers and

Maalox; he slept well, and he found himself losing a lifelong shyness and he was also filled with energy. He has commented that his life and family relations would have been far easier had he learned to relax at a younger age. He often says that his life has been totally revitalized now that he is learning to do deep relaxation.

LIL: What advice would you give to someone looking for a growth group?

GAY: Look for a group leader who has something more than a knowledge of skills. A professional can have all the skills in the world but it is more important to be sensitive and receptive, to be able to facilitate, not to "force" growth. The leader has to be aware of setting the proper pace . . . especially with older people, the pace has to be slower. The leader has to have frequent awareness of the question: What do people in the group need? What do they want?

I think some of the most important qualities to look for in a group is a leader who is honest, able to share his or herself, and who is a growing, searching, real human being.

HEALTHY REMINISCING

A growth group offers an excellent opportunity for breaking out of isolation and loneliness. Breaking *into* isolation, or developing the art of being alone without loneliness, is quite another process. To do this, without feeling abandoned or adrift, requires a solid sense of ourselves and our past. Especially as we get older, reviewing our lives can serve to put our reminiscenses into a tangible, satisfying form.

Reminiscing serves a vital psychological function for people as they grow older. Sometimes we recall past events and people, thoughts, and feelings idly, as daydreams; other times we are purposely trying to remember and reconstruct. Retrospection, either spontaneous or deliberate, is all a part of reminiscence.

Reminiscing about the past is stereotypically considered a sign of mental deterioration, the "meaningless wandering of an aging mind." An older person who talked about the past was immediately characterized as "old" and even "senile"; professionals and family members were likely to react to this "rambling" with indifference, impatience, rejection, or, at best, tolerance. Older people who reminisce are accused of "living in the past" and are devalued. Therapists find it difficult to work with them because it involves a great deal of listening (Butler, 1968). A prevailing tendency among the helping professions has been to identify reminiscence in an older person with psychological dysfunction; it is often regarded as a symptom of pathology.

Recent research offers a new perspective on reminiscence. One of the most thorough studies, by McMahon and Rhudick (1967), explored the relationship between the tendency to reminisce and the degree of mental deterioration and/or depression in their subjects. The research found that (1) reminiscing is not related to one's level of intellectual competence, and (2) older people who can reminisce are *less depressed* than nonreminiscers. Reminiscing has an adaptive function and ". . . appears to be a complex organized mental activity operating under the control of the ego . . . it is positively correlated with successful adaptation . . . through maintaining self-esteem, reaffirming a sense of identity, working through and mastering personal losses and contributing positively to society [p. 78]."

Talking about one's past can be a vital mechanism for staying healthy in the present (Lewis, 1971, p. 243). Stimulating remembrances may help people sustain awareness of themselves and recapture valued parts of their self-image. Memory not only provides continuity, but it is selective in creating and maintaining a sense of personal meaningfulness (McMahon & Rhudick, 1967, p. 73). A healthy person builds a memory bank of experiences throughout life that is a valuable resource in maintaining a sense of his or her worth and interest as an individual.

The best adjusted subjects in the McMahon and Rhudick study used reminiscence for story-telling; past exploits and experiences were recounted with obvious pleasure in a manner that was entertaining. Story-telling can be a way of relating in a meaningful way to other people in the present.

Establishing a secure self-identity based on past experiences, through reminiscing, helps people deal with stress (Lewis, 1973, p. 117). For example, when a woman's husband dies, it may be important for her ". . . to recall all of their life together —both good times and bad—and repeat this reminiscing until memories lose their painfulness. This process is called repetition and working through [Kramer, Kramer, & Dunlop, 1966, p. 16]."

THE THERAPEUTIC ASPECT OF MEMORY

I have used recollection of the past as a powerful form of group therapy in nursing homes. In *reminiscing group therapy* a small group of patients are selected who are able to communicate verbally; I begin by stating that the purpose of the meetings is to share memories. I say something like, "It is very important to look at past events, places, and people in your life. I would like to know more about everyone here, more about your past." All memories are encouraged, and themes or topics are suggested if necessary at the first meeting. Some of the topics I have used include: What do you remember about where you grew up? How did you celebrate holidays and birthdays? What were some of the songs and poems that had special meaning to you? What do you remember about parents, brothers, and sisters?

One of the immediate benefits of reminiscing is potential new friendships. For example, in one group that I led, two men had lived in adjoining hospital rooms for almost six months and had never talked. During group sessions they discovered each other, and found that they shared common experiences. In fact, they had even fought in the same regiment during World War I. A close friendship developed, both men supporting each other in their respective fights to rehabilitate themselves following a stroke. They finally achieved enough health and independence to be able to leave the nursing home and set up a living arrangement together in the community.

Another woman who came to the group was dying of cancer. She was experiencing a great deal of pain and was a "difficult patient" for hospital staff. In the reminiscing group therapy sessions she began to share memories of her only child, a son who had been killed in an accident twenty-five years earlier. She cried not in grief but in guilt for unkind things she had said and done to him; she agonized over having whipped him when he was a child. As she worked through her guilt, her own physical pain diminished. The hospital staff noted not only dramatic changes in her need for pain medication, but also her new serenity, with herself and with others. In talking about her regrets of the past, she was able to find atonement and self-forgiveness through acceptance and support.

THE LIFE REVIEW:
THE PROCESS OF RECORDING

The *life review* is a constructive effort to examine the past as a summation, a history, or an autobiography. It is one of the central tasks of aging. It is a creative process in which you focus on your own internal themes. One purpose of the life review is to experience continuity; it is a quest for meaning in which one reminisces about the past to reorganize for increased self-knowledge in the present.

Socrates, who said "Know thyself," also said, "The unexamined life is not worth living." In order to examine our lives we must have a solid sense of the network of roots that tie us to the past, that support, shape, form, and strengthen us in the present. In the process of a life review, some of our roots may need to be pulled up and discarded; others will be strengthened, perhaps rediscovered. And many will be nourished.

Going back in time can give us perspective as to where we are in the present.

> To be a person is to have a story to tell. We become grounded in the present when we color in the outlines of the past and the future . . . what all persons have in common is their uniqueness. Every person has a story to tell. That's what makes a person.
>
> *[Keen & Fox, 1973, p. 2]*

We live with an incomplete and even compartmentalized sense of self. Many of the threads and roots in each of our lives have gone unobserved. Many tears go unshed, because we were unable to realize our full grief at the time of suffering. Certain periods of life, certain episodes of joy or discovery, are best enjoyed only after they are past.

> Repressed memories . . . won't stay down. To be alive is to have a past. Our only choice is whether we will repress or recreate the past. Childhood may be distant, but it is never quite lost; as full-grown men and women we carry tiny laughing and whimpering children around inside us. We either repress the past and continue to fight its wars with new personnel or we invite it into awareness so that we may see how it has shaped the present.
>
> *[Keen & Fox, 1973, pp. 41–42]*

If we are to make our lives whole, then all the important emotions that belong to us must be felt and integrated (de Castillejo, 1973, p. 157).

The format of each life review is unique and personal. You can write it as a journal, as a memoir, or as an autobiography. Some people prefer to record their story by talking into a tape recorder. Whether written or taped, everyone has the material of a life that could fill at least one book.

The life review is an attempt to permit order to emerge from the many years of experience of the older person (Butler, 1968). The mind rarely photographs; it paints pictures of the past. From these images you select what thoughts, feelings, experiences, and observations are most significant.

Allow yourself to play as you review your life: Seriousness and sobriety do not necessarily aid integration and growth. Play allows for a creative movement to happen as you record.

In accordance with the old folk-saying, "Hindsight has 20/20 vision," we can learn from our past victories or mistakes, pulling together a stronger sense of self.

You may shape your story in many ways. If you already have an idea as to how to organize it, follow that. If not, the following key areas may help you develop your themes. You can use these categories as headings for your story, or simply as areas to think about as you talk or write.

Shaping Events

This section will help you make contact with your life process through time and history. The basic question to ask yourself is: Which experiences have significantly shaped my life?

Some people work best by simply flowing with their thoughts. Initially, do not try to analyze, connect events, or explain happenings. Record the "shaping events" of your life as they occur to you. Then, as a second step, go back to elaborate and trace meanings.

Intellectual Development

What have been the most important influences in your intellectual awakening and development? What have been the most exciting, stimulating, prominent, or powerful forces? Think back to the stepping stones in your mental growth—such as a teacher, a book, a friend, an event, or a poem.

Emotional Development

What have been the potent times of sorrow or loss in your life? What have been the disruptive experiences or events, when you felt sadness or depression? Going back to record points of anguish or grief can be a useful catharsis. By expressing whatever powerful or disruptive emotions we may have bottled up inside us from the past, we discharge tensions; sometimes this leads us to the issues behind such tensions.

The life review is often a good place to think again about someone important to us who has died, who lives in our memories. I often suggest that a person try writing a letter to the deceased, or talk to them using the tape recorder. Try having a conversation with the deceased as if they were still alive. Tell them your thoughts or feelings about them, what you shared together, what you remember about them right now. In what ways do you still miss them? Talk to them directly and tell them.

What have been your deepest experiences of joy, love, peace, and satisfaction? What were the circumstances and surrounding details? What kinds of experiences brought happiness to you? Do you feel that happiness is something you have created and worked for? Or is it mostly spontaneous, an event that simply occurs, a gift? You might want also to review the small moments of pleasure that you have known.

Whether the memories are sad or happy, a life review allows you to express yourself, to restructure your inner experiences, and to realize what has been meaningful and central. The life review is the internal theme in your personal mythology. Many older individuals—both those living in nursing homes and those who are physically healthy and able to live independently —must see themselves as part of a significant spot in history. Remembering his or her own contributions to human history enhances a person's sense of dignity and integrity, and it heightens the awareness of individuality and uniqueness, which leads to a sense of wholeness.

Older people can sometimes experience what young people cannot: a personal sense of a total life experience. A young person will often keep a daily personal journal; an older person, however, is in a position to incorporate more of a sense of history in his or her autobiography. Many people become more deeply interested in religion and philosophy as they age; in Japan, older people commonly write poetry as an expression of personal life meaning.

The life review elucidates your personal mythology. It is a chance to record your existence, to integrate historical experiences, and to construct a valuable personal identity. It can be a small spot of immortality in which you know, "I have existed; my life has mattered."

CHOOSING DIRECTIONS FOR ENERGY: A PERSONAL MYTHOLOGY

How do we use our energy as we grow older?

Some people deny that they have less energy and they try to maintain, at all costs and without differentiation, their involvements. They react to aging by increasing their activity, as if to prove themselves. They step up their investments of energy and often overdraw themselves, at the expense of their health, not to mention some of their commitments. Overextended, they feel frustrated at trying to keep up; they may have a physical sense of "being burned out."

Other people run away from the unknowns of an aging body and uncertain health by disengaging themselves from life. In withdrawing their energy and commitments, they pay the penalty of less aliveness, less creativity—and often boredom.

Others fluctuate between these two extremes of overcommitment and withdrawal, compulsively bouncing back and forth.

Perhaps the wisest solution to the reality of decreasing energy is to make *selective* and *conscious use of time* in ways that are satisfying but not depleting. In response to the change in our energy levels, we can reorganize our lives on simpler levels. Our bodies function as integral parts of ourselves when we respond to physical cues. In our teens, although few of us were conscious of what we did, we managed to integrate our many changes—in the course of many mistakes and wasted energy. As we grow older we have to adjust to less energy and probably some aches and pains. At this time, we can take charge of our lives and make deliberate choices on how we use our energy.

How you choose to spend your time and energy determines the content of your life. Hopefully you will make your choices deliberately and thoughtfully, rather than being swept along or drifting into them. One way to begin the process of deciding how to live in the present is by increasing your self-knowledge through an examination of how you have come to be. Your decisions and behaviors are consistent for the person who has been there throughout. Gathering up the facts and emotions of your life, deriving an outline of your story's plot, can show you your purpose and constancy.

In a sense, we all have personal generation gaps to span. We all live with a family of different selves: some are less acceptable; some have been disowned; or some are mere acquaintances. This unique combination of selves—who you are—will never exist again in history. An old Jewish proverb describes the challenge: "If I am not fully myself, if I try to be something less or like someone else, then who will be like me?"

THE SENSE OF DISCOVERY

The elderly mountain-climber had a remarkable sense of discovery. Her type of openness to new experience tends to get lost in the adult years, in the scramble to work and to build security. Society assigns the period of learning and discovery to youth. The inquiring and exploring roles are discouraged as a major part of adult living.

As you become an adult, you master the skills and activities for assuming responsibilities; discovery gives way to repetition and to the maintenance of acquisitions. Adults learn efficiency in performing their work; yet efficiency does not necessarily release you for continuing the adventure of discovery. Instead, you are subject to habit—getting into ruts and building exclusively for the future—rather than adventuring into the present.

As Maslow points out, self-actualization is a dynamic, ongoing process. Whether through a growth group, a life review, or other ways of adventuring (including reading this book), you need to cultivate and treasure a sense of being on the frontier of living.

To continue to discover and grow makes for a life of adventure and wonder!

Four

PREVENTION OF PHYSICAL DETERIORATION: CHOOSING HEALTHY HABITS

Most of us in America today are born with bodies that are guaranteed for 75 years or more of healthy living. But how many of us bother to read the maintenance instructions on that warranty? How seriously do we regard the conditions? The physical manifestations of aging appear only gradually: wrinkles appear slowly; the skin dries out year by year; the hair turns gray and thins out much later. At such a gradual pace, we can easily repress the reality of even the visible changes.

Internally, the inexorable deterioration goes on as well: The blood vessels become less limber, and the heart and lungs are steadily less efficient. Kidney functioning is greatly reduced, and the bladder loses capacity and control. The brain shrinks. The production of hormones lessens. As muscles shrink and weaken, joints stiffen and swell. Vision dims as the lenses of the eyes thicken and become opaque. Hearing grows less sensitive. Fat accumulates on the body, usually at the midsection. And the cells, the basic unit of life, decline in their ability to function.

Yet we live each day as if health were ensured forever.

The anxiety produced by aging can be a positive motivating force to take better care of ourselves. Despite the inevitability of changes with age, *much can be done to slow down the course of the aging process and to promote health.* Just as you can extend the life of a machine with proper maintenance and care, so can you encourage your health.

Health maintenance should start early—at least by the middle years. A 56-year-old woman came to see me for psychotherapy. Her husband had left her; her children were living independent lives and no longer needed her. Helen's primary concern in seeking professional help was to learn how to live alone and find new goals, after being a housewife all her adult years. However, she was also alarmed by her physical status. Recently, for the first time in years, Helen had taken a good, long look at herself in the mirror: She noticed the sagging skin on her underarms, and her thicker waistline; she also became aware of a shortness of breath and stiffness in some joints. For years she had been promising herself that "tomorrow" she would take time off and do something about her neglected self. "Is it too late for me?" she asked.

Although Helen started late and had a poorly developed sense of herself, her motivation was unusually high. The discipline of her new interest in self-care added purpose to her days. She found pleasure in the recreating of herself. Though it took over a year, she was able to improve both her appearance and her health.

It had taken years of neglect for Helen to bring about her unsatisfactory physical condition. Fortunately, it took less time to reclaim her body and health.

However, you should not let yourself go as long as Helen did. The time to prepare for healthy aging is at the age of thirty or earlier. The fall-out on poor self-care may be as much as twenty years later, and repairing the damage is not always possible.

PREVENTION VERSUS CURING

In ancient Greece, two goddesses ruled over health. Panakeia represented the treatment of disease and presided over the use of medication; her sister, the goddess Hygeia, was the preserver of health. Hygeia represented, in modern terminology, health maintenance through the teaching of techniques for a "sound mind in a sound body." Many people opt for healing medication (Panakeia) rather than taking the time and energy to stay healthy.

Health is so abstract and intangible—so "normal" you might say—that you are most aware of it only in its absence. When you fall ill, you often react with fear and sorrow; but since fear is usually too overwhelming to live with, after a while you find a way to repress it. For example, in Reno, Nevada, men who survive heart attacks are referred by their physicians to a Physical Stress Reduction Program in which they are taught to integrate psychological and physical methods to reduce stress factors in their lives, as stress' relation to heart disease is well established. The men are instructed in relaxation, body- and self-awareness techniques, exercise, and diet. Above all, emphasis is placed on their need to change their lifestyles, so they will give time on a regular, daily basis to relaxation and good health habits.

Heart patients come to the program afraid for their lives; initially they are highly motivated to improve their self-care. However, the fear wears off—and the vast majority of these men fail to maintain any permanent changes in lifestyle. After several months they come to believe that they have "beaten the odds," that everything is normal again (despite medical information to the contrary), and they drop out of the program. Those who remain, on the other hand, greatly increase their chances for healthy survival.

FEELING GOOD AND "WELL-AGING"

The goddess Hygeia is most successful in her teachings when you realize that taking good care of yourself can make you feel good. The person who exercises regularly will find that the body craves those sensations: *good health is the ultimate expression of the joy of living.* Health is not only the absence of disease, but it is also the creative ability to live well with body awareness and sensitivity. By paying attention to your body, you become aware of the body signals that constitute your personal guide to health. You need to be sensitive to these signals and willing to heed them. How often have we all ignored our internal voices?

Maintaining health means living with integrity and according to our life needs. Some health professionals now theorize, for example, that sustained guilt or rage can cause cancer (Silverman, 1973). Maintaining health is work. "An apple a day" won't do it. Nor will a pill or three minutes of daily exercise. Health is part of a total style of living. It is being able to relax and to permit yourself pleasure. It means seeking balance and flexibility and strength. Health is allowing yourself to feel deeply. It is being able to fight when necessary, to protect yourself, and to "let go" at appropriate times. It means staying away from toxic people and environments. In this sense, *health of the body is dependent on a healthy mind, the mind that creates the environment that nourishes us as a totality.* However, even with a sound ecology of mind-body-environment, you still need the teachings of Hygeia—the knowledge of how to best promote health.

We therefore need to match our well-baby clinics with well-aging clinics that offer health education throughout adult life. Recent scientific findings offer excellent suggestions for postponing the familiar bodily decrements and for maintaining health. Physical aging, the summation of physiologic processes occurring throughout a lifetime, is responsive to environmental modification.

PHYSICAL EXERCISE AND AGING

Longevity is clearly multifactorial; that is, no single factor stops the aging process. However, experts agree on a number of factors important to health that can be enhanced through "well-aging" education:

1. exercise and physical activity;
2. diet, nutrition, and staying slender;
3. psychological factors of lifestyle, stress, psychosomatic health, and self-concept;
4. social factors of status and retirement; and
5. environmental factors.

This chapter examines the areas of exercise, diet, and personal habits (items 1 and 2); Chapter 5 treats the remaining areas of well-aging.

The Benefits of Physical Exercise

Morehouse (1975) estimates that 80 percent of American adults "do not exercise properly for stopping physiological decay [p. 18]."

Before we discuss specifics, imagine the following: A drug company has developed a new medication, a pill that protects your heart, increases your energy, helps you sleep better, solves your weight problem, and stops many of the decrements associated with aging. This magic pill offers:

- increased resiliency and suppleness of the arteries;
- greatly increased protection against the likelihood of heart attack, and much increased chance of survival should one occur;
- sustained capacity of lungs and respiratory reserves;
- less accumulation of fat;
- maintenance of physical flexibility, balance, agility, and reaction time;
- greatly preserved muscle strength;
- protection against ligamentous injuries;
- greatly increased safeguards against dislocation strains in the knees, spine, and shoulders;
- the basal metabolic rates sustained to a greater degree;
- improved peripheral resistance, blood cholesterol, and blood pressure; and
- shielding against the occurrence of bone fractures, caused by bone brittleness, demineralization and porousness.

This magical medication is now available! However, it is not a pill or medication. . . . It is exercise.

Exercise is the closest thing to an anti-aging and anti-disease pill. The fountain of youth for which Ponce de Leon searched the world was inside his own body. "Exercise is the means to an alert, vigorous and lengthy life . . . an inactive life is a slow form of suicide [Morehouse, 1975, p. 21]." Research indicates that exercise significantly increases the likelihood of good health and long life. For example, in Leaf's 1973 study of British postal workers, those who delivered the mail were compared to their colleagues who worked at office desks: The mail carriers who walked many miles a day had a significantly lower incidence of heart attacks (p. 49). In a related study, English bus drivers and bus conductors were observed: The conductors, who spent their working day walking up and down the stairs of London's double-deck buses, had much less heart disease than the bus drivers (Leaf, p. 50).

"You are as old as your arteries [Bahr, 1972, p. 104]." If an individual lives a sedentary life, his/her blood vessels thicken with plaque and the vessels themselves narrow; the blood must then work harder to circulate. This process, called *peripheral resistance,* results in increased blood pressure and ultimately can lead to heart failure.

Maintaining artery flexibility is "one of the most dramatic areas in which physical activity can keep the body relatively youthful [p. 104]." Dr. Herbert A. deVries of the University of Southern California found in testing men between the ages of 52 and 88 that exercise, such as brisk walking and jogging, can improve heart and blood-vessel functioning significantly. In another study (Kaluger & Kaluger, 1974) of 125 retired men, exercise caused dramatic improvement in physical conditioning (p. 301). Circulatory and cardiac function improved significantly even in a group of sedentary older people with an average age of 70 who exercised regularly for three months (Barry, 1966, p. 182).

Hundreds of studies conclude that endurance exercises improve cardiovascular functioning (Bahr, 1972, p. 105). The heart, circulation, and respiratory functioning are all improved by endurance exercises, such as long walks, jogging, swimming, cross-country skiing, and bicycle riding. The American Medical Joggers Association, a group organized by physicians, conducted a study in which not a single case of coronary heart disease appeared among marathon runners (Leaf, 1975, p. 106). Morehouse (1975) writes that cardiologists recommend exercise for the prevention of heart disease and that "every cardiologist I know is exercising [p. 80]."

Men who exercised regularly were also found to have higher intelligence scores (Powell & Pohndorf, 1971, p. 70). Improved intellectual functioning could be related to the increased oxygen supply to the brain and to the differences in blood pressure, both of which benefit by exercise.

Physical activity is also good for our bones. Exercise balances bone formation and destruction, helping the bones to remain mineralized, dense, and strong. "With inactivity at any age our bones lose their calcium salts and become thin and fragile, just as our muscles atrophy and become smaller and weaker with disuse [Leaf, 1975, p. 104]."

Americans are just about *past* the stage of being sedentary —to the point of immobility (Emhart, 1973, p. 122). Most of us work all day sitting down. We spend our leisure time watching TV and driving in automobiles, instead of walking. One probable result: American men have a shorter life expectancy than men in other Western industrialized nations. Men in our country will live, on the average, several years less than, for example, their Norwegian counterparts. Dietary differences between the two countries are not significant, but there are marked differences in physical activity and lifestyle. The Norwegian who sits at a desk all week plans his entire weekend in the mountains, either hiking or cross-country skiing. This attitude represents the Norwegian's ability to relax, take regular time off away from work, and change the tempo of living to include pleasuring.

Be realistic in planning a health regimen for yourself. An exercise program that is too abrupt and demanding will become a dreaded part of your day rather than a pleasure. Too often people embark on exercise programs as if they are "crash" diets—superhuman programs at which the ordinary person can only fail.

In working out an exercise program, set your standards low enough to be comfortable. Be contented with less, rather than force yourself into something you dislike. The important thing is to set up an exercise program that is pleasurable, so that you'll stay with it. Life has enough burdens without adding to the list. The purpose of exercise should be pleasure, not punishment. If you enjoy swimming, swim three times a week instead of forcing yourself to swim every day.

Body movement (or exercise) can develop into a *need* —an acute physical pleasure, a sensitivity to the physical desire to stretch, flex, and experience the power of your body.

Most older persons are not preoccupied with health and diet, in spite of the stereotype. As one old timer said:

I refuse to worry about what to eat and do . . . Who wants to live to be a hundred, anyway? What's the point? I've always felt that I'd rather have a short and busy life than a long, dull one—especially if living a long time meant living in fear, with caution, worry, and perpetual doctors hanging around.

This 85-year-old man—who regularly horseback rides five hours a day!—embodies the desire and attitude of being vigorous. Such energy almost always finds expression in some form of physical activity that is enjoyed for itself.

Maximize your physical *pleasure.* In so doing, you will also maintain your health while enjoying yourself.

The stereotype of growing older dictates that our bodies will grow rigid and fragile. Accordingly, we rob old age of its natural dignity by assigning it to rocking chairs. The older person who sits down or stops trying is done for. You don't have to be that way, but if you want to wind up in a wheelchair by the age of 60, then don't exercise! In 400 B.C., Hippocrates said, "That which you do not use, you lose." This applies to the mind, to the soul, and to the body as well.

By middle-age a person can begin to fully develop his or her agility, gracefulness, and centeredness. The physically active person learns to balance, to conserve, and to concentrate strength—valuable lessons that carry over to the rest of living. Exercise is sterile only if our attitude is. Our bodies can age gracefully, with flexibility and agility. With continuing care, the person of 65 or 70 can often enjoy the good health previously associated with middle-age.

Physical exercise—whether it is folk dancing, Tai Chi, ballet, walking, jogging, or calisthenics—can also take on a meditative quality. The commingling of mind and body involvement massages the spirit, awakening a sense of the life-force flowing throughout all of nature.

Try exercising as a type of meditation, by concentrating strictly on your specific activity. Make it an experience of total absorption. As you exercise, focus on yourself: your breathing, your body muscles, the gentle stretching of your joints, your foot touching the ground, and the feeling of air on the surface of your skin.

You cannot concentrate exclusively on your activity if you are distracted by your duties. Set the day's work aside as you exercise. Concentrate on your body in the here-and-now. Make it a sensuous activity. Some people find it useful to keep a notepad close by while exercising. If your thoughts are constantly drawn to the work that needs to be done, make a note of it; knowing that you've written it down often helps to clear your mind.

Your initiative and self-motivation will get you going. No one can make you save these moments for yourself. You have to decide for yourself what is important and how to use your time and energy. If your schedule doesn't include time for pleasures and self-care, then it's up to you to change your lifestyle. You can always find the time for the things you really want to do. The question becomes: How much of a priority are you to yourself?

The Type of Exercise for You

We know that heart, respiratory, urinary, neuromuscular, skeletal, and nervous systems all deteriorate rapidly during prolonged disuse (Winter, 1973, p. 95). However, the exact kind and extent of exercise needed to counter this deterioration are still controversial questions.

There are two general categories of exercise, both of which are necessary. One broad classification includes body movements affecting skeletal muscle strength and flexibility; these exercises keep your muscles toned and able to perform a range of motions, but do not condition the heart, circulation, and lungs. The other category is primarily for increasing the efficiency of the heart, respiratory, and circulatory systems; these exercises, such as swimming or hiking, have a small but limited effect on skeletal muscles.

Strength and flexibility exercises. Isometrics, weight lifting, calisthenics, and body movement exercises have specific effects on skeletal muscles. These exercises need to be tailored to fit your individual interests, preferences, and needs. A number of excellent books suggest a wide range of these muscular exercises (Craig, 1968; Kuntzleman, 1971; Lurie & Segev, 1969; Morehouse, 1975; Royal Canadian Air Force, 1962).

Choose both muscle-building and body-flexibility exercises, including at least one exercise for arm strengthening and one for abdominal muscle strengthening. Several general guidelines apply to all exercises:

1. Never bounce or jerk your muscles when exercising. Stretch gently. All movements should be slow, moderate, and smooth. Exercises should be done rhythmically, whether you are stretching or flexing. The strengthening and the stretching of muscles should be a dance of flowing movement.

2. Effort and pain should be minimal. Sore muscles or joint pain are signs of exercising too hard or trying to progress too fast. Start slowly and progress slowly.

3. Don't do strenuous exercise for at least two hours after eating a meal.

4. Never force any movement so that a muscle feels strained.

5. Many calisthenic exercises used in gym classes or taught by inexperienced teachers are bad for your back or knees. They do more harm than good. *Avoid* the following:

   a. Standing with your legs straight and reaching over to try to touch your toes. This can cause a strained back. (As a rule, try not to stand with your knees locked. Your knees should be slightly bent, whether exercising or going about routine living.)

   b. Push-ups and double leg raises can hurt the back unless you are already in good physical condition.

   c. Sit-ups should only be done by using a curling motion, with your feet free and your knees slightly flexed. The second half of the exercise, going from the sitting position down to the floor, is the most important. Start with your chest at your knees. Go backwards very slowly. With your hands, feel your abdominal muscles and make sure you're putting them to work. The tendency is to use your hip flexor muscles instead of abdominal muscles. As you go backwards, slowly toward the floor, feel your muscles; half-way down to the floor hold the position for as long as you can until they begin to quiver. Work for the strength to hold for several seconds.

    d. Deep knee-bends should be avoided because they can cause knee problems with aging.

Some very specific kinds of exercise may become advisable as one grows older, especially for improving balance, strengthening of the urinary control muscles, and reducing back problems.

Agility, flexibility, reaction time, and balance are greatly enhanced by physical activity. With aging, a sense of balance is particularly important. Older people are more likely to fall and injure themselves because decreased activity can result in a loss of a sense of balance. This problem is sometimes compounded by the frequent use of aspirin, usually taken to help arthritic pain. Aspirin affects the middle ear and hearing ability, which drastically hinders balance.

For most people improved balance is an automatic bonus for doing any kind of exercise. For others, programming exercises that specifically affect the sense of balance may be necessary. Yoga is one excellent way to increase both flexibility and balance. It combines three techniques—concentration, relaxation, and stretching—to produce sensitivity, calmness, and balance.

Endurance exercises. The second, extremely important category of exercise essentially are those that require oxygen and endurance. Running, swimming, cycling, and brisk walking all have an effect on the heart and lungs. These exercises are important for men at any age and for women after the age of 40. While a greater and earlier incidence of heart disease occurs in men, after the age of 40 a woman's arteries become disabled even faster than a man's. Bricklin (1973) observes that "whatever natural protection a woman has against heart disease begins to disappear at a very rapid rate [p. 135]." Equally important for both men and women is that regular endurance exercise reduces high blood pressure and serum cholesterol (Bricklin, 1973, p. 135). Other changes that occur as a result of vigorous exercise are:

- increased efficiency of the lungs to process more aid with less effort;
- greater heart strength to pump more blood with each stroke;
- increased xmxmxmmxmxmxmmxmxmxmxmxmxmxmxmxmxmx
- increased size and number of blood vessels;
- increased blood volume;
- increased tone of muscles and blood vessels; and
- improved oxygen consumption (Cooper & Cooper, 1968, p. 28).

When a skeletal muscle is exercised, it grows stronger. Likewise, when the heart is exercised, it grows stronger. The condition of the skeletal muscles is measured in terms of strength and endurance. With the heart, improvement is determined by a reduced resting pulse rate, a lower pulse rate when under physical stress, and a faster rate of recovery after exercising.

The United States space program has found, in helping astronauts to stay fit during space flights, that the most important physiological signal to monitor is the heart rate (Morehouse, 1975, p. 26). The key is your pulse rate. It must be pushed up high enough and held there long enough for cardiovascular conditioning to take place.

It is important to warm up before commencing an active sport, as heart rate and dilation of blood vessels have to adapt to the increased activity. Stretching exercises and calisthenics are ways to warm up.

Which type of vigorous exercise you choose is not the critical factor. Any activity that increases the pulse rate to at least 120 is beneficial. Pick whatever you enjoy and whatever is convenient, but also experiment with different activities.

(One word of incidental caution to joggers: Jogging downhill puts an immense strain on your knees. Run only on level ground or uphill. If possible, run on grass or earth, rather than on concrete. Also, try to stay away from heavily trafficked streets where you must breathe exhaust fumes.)

No exercise offers a layaway plan. You can't store up physical fitness. The consensus among the experts as to the amount of exercise necessary to prevent deterioration with aging is that muscular strengthening and stretching exercises must be done at least fifteen minutes, three times weekly on nonconsecutive days (Maness, 1976, p. 130). How long you should sustain vigorous exercise for heart and circulation depends on what you do.

Doing It

For many people, the difficult part of exercising is not deciding what to do or how much, but rather doing it on a continuing and regular schedule. The small emergencies of daily living push aside self-care programs, unless you structure this time into a routine. For example, one of my colleagues goes to the YWCA for an exercise class several times a week during her noon hour. Another person, who works at home, exercises before nine every morning. Others who prefer to exercise in the evening set aside time before dinner every night. But without a time-frame, without a part of the day committed to exercising, you can keep postponing it until "just one more thing is done." Eventually, your program has been procrastinated out of existence.

In addition to structuring a time, a written record of what you are doing often helps your memory and motivation. One of the excellent features of the Canadian Air Force Booklet on isometric and cardiovascular exercise routines (which has sold millions of copies) is a layout in which you keep a record of progress. Even once you attain the exercise level you wish to maintain, keeping a record for review at the end of a month is helpful. I also recommend recording your weight at the beginning of each month, as one measure of the effectiveness of your program.

The success or failure of an exercise program depends on how much you enjoy it. Experiment, discover what you enjoy, and make it part of your living. If your exercise program is not a happy experience, it needs modification.

While exercise works best as part of your daily routine, generally speaking it is best not to exercise when you are ill or exhausted, either physically or emotionally. If you are worried about a problem and feel wrung-out from the stress, then exercise may not be the right thing. On the other hand, exercise sometimes integrates mind and body when they are at odds. If in doubt, try it and see how it goes. Learn to distinguish between a disinclination to exercise and ill health.

Concentrating your energy into one activity, such as running, can be a form of relaxation. Physical activity can be therapeutic; it can pull together the scattered pieces of your life. A crucial part of a well-aging attitude is to help yourself incorporate regular exercise into daily living, even to the extent of maintaining a program when under pressure or work demands. A lack of exercise and activity is likely to reduce the ability to withstand stress and may reduce integration of mind and body (Kuntzleman, 1971, p. 390). Even while vacationing, you can find time for self-care. The challenge is to make exercise a real part of the rest of your life—even with life's fluctuations, demands, and complexities.

DIET AND NUTRITION

The centenarians of Hunza, Vilcabamba, and the Caucasus maintain diets low in animal fats and under two thousand calories a day. Americans, by contrast, average thirty-three hundred calories a day, including large quantities of fat. The best-informed medical opinion is that this amount of intake is excessive (Leaf, 1973, p. 49). Americans eat too much, and they eat the wrong foods, which contribute to poor health and a shorter life.

An old folk saying states: The wider the waistline, the shorter the lifeline. Extra weight puts a burden on the heart. Every pound of fat requires an expanded system of blood vessels, which in turn requires the heart to pump extra gallons of blood over longer distances. Obesity is one of the chief factors contributing to heart disease, the number one killer in the United States.

The Michigan Heart Association has developed a test you can take, to alert yourself to your personal risk of having a heart attack. The test is shown in Figure 4-1. The results provide an estimate of your current danger. Each question represents a risk factor of conditions and habits associated with heart attack. To take the test, study each risk factor question; then find the box applicable to you in each horizontal row and circle the large number in it. For example, if you are 37, circle the number in the box labeled "31–40."

This test does not measure all the risk factors of heart disease. According to a scale developed by the Heart Association, additional factors that greatly increase the danger of heart attack are:

1. Your character or personality, and the stress under which you live—an extremely significant factor discussed in the next chapter.
2. Diabetes, particularly when present for many years.
3. Your vital capacity in breathing. Vital capacity is determined by measuring the amount of air you can take into your lungs in proportion to the size of your lungs. The less air you can breathe, the higher your risk. This capacity is usually reduced by smoking.
4. Your electrocardiogram. If certain abnormalities are present in the record of the electrical currents generated by your heart, you have a higher risk. This factor is the least subject to change. However, diet and exercise can still be crucial in maintaining health and preventing deterioration. A person who is aware of a heart abnormality can allow for necessary adjustments in daily living patterns.

RISKO

The purpose of this game is to give you an estimate of your chances of suffering heart attack.

The game is played by making squares which — from left to right — represent an increase in your RISK FACTORS. These are medical conditions and habits associated with an increased danger of heart attack. Not all risk factors are measurable enough to be included in this game; see back of sheet for other RISK FACTORS.

RULES:

Study each RISK FACTOR AND its row. Find the box applicable to you and circle the large number in it. For example, if you are 37, circle the number in the box labeled 31-40. After checking out all the rows, add the circled numbers. This total — your score — is an estimate of your risk.

IF YOU SCORE:

6-11 — Risk well below average	25-31 — Risk moderate
12-17 — Risk below average	32-40 — Risk at a dangerous level
18-24 — Risk generally average	41-62 — Danger urgent. See your doctor now.

HEREDITY:
Count parents, grand-parents, brothers, and sisters who have had heart attack and/or stroke.

TOBACCO SMOKING:
If you inhale deeply and smoke a cigarette way down, add one to your classification. Do NOT subtract because you think you do not inhale or smoke only a half inch on a cigarette.

EXERCISE:
Lower your score one point if you exercise regularly and frequently.

CHOLESTEROL OR SATURATED FAT INTAKE LEVEL:
A cholesterol blood level is best. If you can't get one from your doctor, then estimate the percentage of solid fats you eat. These are usually of animal origin — lard, cream, butter, and beef and lamb fat. If you eat much of this, your cholesterol level probably will be high. The U.S. average, 40%, is too high for good health.

BLOOD PRESSURE:
If you have no recent reading but have passed an insurance or industrial examination chances are your reading 140 or less.

SEX:
This line takes into account the fact that men have from 6 to 10 times more heart attacks than women of child bearing age.

	10 to 20 (1)	21 to 30 (2)	31 to 40 (3)	41 to 50 (4)	51 to 60 (6)	61 to 70 and over (7)
AGE	10 to 20	21 to 30	31 to 40	41 to 50	51 to 60	61 to 70 and over
HEREDITY	No known history of heart disease	1 relative with cardiovascular disease Over 60	2 relatives with cardiovascular disease Over 60	1 relative with cardiovascular disease Under 60	2 relatives with cardiovascular disease Under 60	3 relatives with cardiovascular disease Under 60
WEIGHT	More than 5 lbs. below standard weight	-5 to +5 lbs. standard weight	6-20 lbs. over weight	21-35 lbs. over weight	36-50 lbs. over weight	51-65 lbs. over weight
TOBACCO SMOKING	Non-user	Cigar and/or pipe	10 cigarettes or less a day	20 cigarettes a day	30 cigarettes a day	40 cigarettes a day or more
EXERCISE	Intensive occupational and recreational exertion	Moderate occupational and recreational exertion	Sedentary work and intense recreational exertion	Sedentary occupational and moderate recreational exertion	Sedentary work and light recreational exertion	Complete lack of all exercise
CHOLESTEROL OR FAT % IN DIET	Cholesterol below 180 mg.% Diet contains no animal or solid fats	Cholesterol 181-205 mg.% Diet contains 10% animal or solid fats	Cholesterol 206-230 mg.% Diet contains 20% animal or solid fats	Cholesterol 231-255 mg.% Diet contains 30% animal or solid fats	Cholesterol 256-280 mg.% Diet contains 40% animal or solid fats	Cholesterol 281-300 mg.% Diet contains 50% animal or solid fats
BLOOD PRESSURE	100 upper reading	120 upper reading	140 upper reading	160 upper reading	180 upper reading	200 or over upper reading
SEX	Female under 40	Female 40-50	Female over 50	Male	Stocky male	Bald stocky male

© MICHIGAN HEART ASSOCIATION
69

Figure 4-1. RISKO—The Michigan Heart Association Test. © Michigan Heart Association.

Because of the difficulty in measuring them, these RISK FACTORS are not included in "RISKO":

Diabetes, particularly when present for many years.

Your Character or Personality, and the *Stress* under which you live.

Vital Capacity — determined by measuring the amount of air you can take into your lungs in proportion to the size of your lungs. The less air you can breathe, the higher your risk.

Electrocardiogram — if certain abnormalities are present in the record of the electrical currents generated by your heart you have a higher risk.

Gout — is caused by a higher than normal amount of uric acid in the blood. Patients have an increased risk.

IF YOU HAVE A NUMBER OF RISK FACTORS, FOR THE SAKE OF YOUR HEALTH, ASK YOUR DOCTOR TO CHECK YOUR MEDICAL CONDITIONS AND QUIT YOUR RISK FACTOR HABITS.

NOTE: The fact that various habits or conditions may be rated similarly in this test does not mean these are of equal risk. The reaction of individual human beings to Risk Factors — as to many other things — is so varied it is impossible to draw valid conclusions for any individual.

This scale has been developed only to highlight what the Risk Factors are and what can be done about them. It is not designed to be a medical diagnosis.

5. Gout, which is caused by a higher-than-normal amount of uric acid in the blood. People with gout have an increased risk. This can be greatly improved and even eliminated through proper diet.

Many physicians believe that obesity is the single greatest deterrent to increased life span. Carrying extra weight predisposes a person toward the development of a number of diseases and health problems besides heart failure. High blood pressure, arteriosclerosis, diabetes, pneumonia, gallbladder disease, intestinal problems, constipation, varicose veins, and hernia are all conditions common to obesity (Rothenberg, 1964, p. 670). Obesity also increases the risk of dying in the event of surgery.

The scientific evidence about the importance of a low-fat diet is convincing. And yet why is one out of every five Americans overweight? Why don't the majority of adults practice what they believe to be healthful eating? Perhaps because poor nutritional habits constitute such a complex problem in treating obesity, the medical profession is a self-confessed failure (Johnson, 1973, p. 146). Medically prescribed diets achieve a long-run (two years or more) success rate of only 2 percent. With the help of diet pills and/or the usual food-deprivation diet (counting calories, cutting carbohydrates, eating meat only, and so on), people lose weight. However, recent medical statistics show that a full 98 percent of these dieters regain their original weight within two years (Waxler, 1971, p. 351–355).

Diet pills have dangerous side effects and just don't work in the long run. Restrictive diet schemes, based on willpower and self-denial, don't work either; in fact, a person who uses diet pills and goes on a medically prescribed diet usually continues to gain weight. One dieter told me: "Over the past three years I've lost one hundred pounds by various diets—and I've regained one hundred and ten pounds."

The word "diet" originated from the Latin word *diæta,* meaning "a manner of living." How and what you eat is a personal matter, determined by your taste preferences, food associations to the past, finances, personality, metabolism, physical size, activity patterns, and digestive system. To follow a prescribed diet usually means adhering to an artificial manner of living not of your own making.

This is the dilemma of dieting. You need to feed your emotions, as well as your body. Food is one of life's greatest pleasures and comforts. Most diets do not allow for food pleasures or your food-related psychological needs. A deprivational diet ignores the emotional values of eating. When the psychological needs become overwhelming, the dieter goes on a binge, "blows the diet," gains weight, becomes depressed and guilty, and needs the comfort of food even more. And so the vicious cycle goes.

Creating Your Own Diet

If you have a weight problem, try creating your own diet and allow it to be flexible. First of all, increase your awareness of your manner of living—the ways you use food and the times you eat. Once you accept the fact that eating gives you psychological satisfaction and fulfills emotional needs, your diet must take this admission into account. Eating must serve many needs, including pleasure, in order for weight problems to be permanently resolved.

Study your habits. Habits can prevent you from eating according to your body wisdom. For example, do you automatically eat just because it's a certain time of day? Do you eat only the kinds and amounts of food you want? Or were you taught to habitually "clean your plate?"

Make yourself conscious of eating. What did you eat for dinner last night? If you can't remember, perhaps you're eating in an automatic way, without paying attention to the meal or its sensations. When eating does not offer pleasure and physiological satisfaction, it is wasteful and inefficient. You need only a small amount of food for physiological satisfaction; when you've been cheated of the pleasure of eating, you end up eating much more than you need. The time to eat is when you are hungry and when you can enjoy the sensations of eating, without distractions or tensions. For example, trying to eat at a large dinner party, talking to people and watching what's going on—it is often impossible to concentrate on food sensations. As a result, you will often eat another meal of snacks when you get home.

Food represents nourishment, medicine, habit, tradition, social contact, emotional security, entertainment, comfort, pleasurable sensation, and other psychological needs. Considering that we need to pack all of this into about two thousand calories a day, no wonder people overeat so easily!

Complicating the older person's problem is the plain medical fact that basal metabolism declines with aging, which means that less food is required (Table 4–1). After approximately the age of 30, we need to gradually reduce our food intake to adjust to our declining metabolism. Otherwise, we will gain weight. Even if you exercise the same amount, you must decrease your food consumption by at least 10 percent to keep your weight normal (Rothenberg, 1964, p. 668).

As you grow older and are thus allowed fewer calories, awareness of your individual food needs is increasingly important. Traditionally, the approach to food has been puritanical. People put themselves on diets, figure out nutritional needs,

Calorie Allowance for Adults of Average Physical Activity*

	Desirable Weight in Pounds	*Calorie Allowance*		
		25 Years	*45 Years*	*65 Years*
MEN:	110	2,300	2,050	1,750
	120	2,400	2,200	1,850
	130	2,550	2,300	1,950
	140	2,700	2,450	2,050
	150	2,850	2,550	2,150
	160	3,000	2,700	2,250
	170	3,100	2,800	2,350
	180	3,250	2,950	2,450
	190	3,400	3,050	2,600
WOMEN:	100	1,750	1,600	1,350
	110	1,900	1,700	1,450
	120	2,000	1,800	1,500
	130	2,100	1,900	1,600
	140	2,250	2,050	1,700
	150	2,350	2,150	1,800
	160	2,500	2,250	1,900

*American Medical Association data.

and schedule convenient times of the day for eating. Unfortunately, this approach overlooks the part of eating that has to do with your psychological moods and your need for pleasuring yourself.

If you have to diet, then restrict your calories by balancing a combination of nutritional needs with your other food needs. Recognize that food cravings are normal and legitimate. One of the paradoxes about dieting is that people put themselves into a prison of restrictions; eventually they break out and eat the foods they crave, but they feel so guilty about doing so that they end up having to eat more to enjoy the sensations. The joy of eating, like sex, can become blocked or dulled by guilt. One of the most successful ways of losing weight, therefore, is by liberating yourself from guilt and by giving yourself permission to enjoy your food cravings. Have a love affair with food—don't rape it! Don't allow your "surrender" to be followed by gorging. Most weight problems have to do with the *amount* you eat, not *what* you eat.

In general, advice about diet and nutrition applies uniformly to people young or old (Rothenberg, 1964, p. 207). We are composed of what we eat. Good food is essential to good health at any age. However, with aging, moderation becomes essential. The aging body becomes increasingly sensitive to and less tolerant of poor food habits.

CHOOSING HEALTH

We have been discussing ways of slowing down the course of physical aging and promoting health. Adult health information is important for self-care. However, bodily health is dependent on a healthy mind that chooses which information to apply and which living style to create.

According to Dr. Belloc (1973), at the California Department of Health and Human Population Laboratory, the results of a ten-year study indicate that men who follow seven "golden rules" of health practice live up to an average of eleven years longer than men who follow three or fewer; women who follow the practices will outlive their contemporaries who don't by seven years. The "golden rules" are, in brief:

1. drink moderately,
2. maintain normal weight,
3. no smoking,
4. exercise regularly,
5. maintain a good diet,
6. get enough rest, and
7. develop healthy food habits.

Other studies (Dill & Wasserman, 1964; Palmore, 1969) conclude that whether a person *practices* the "golden rules" is a question related to life satisfaction, to the ability to experience happiness, and to adeptness in relaxing.

Learning how to live with stress and to create a healthy living style in our modern society is probably as important a part of health education as exercising and good dietary habits. In the next chapter we will look at stress, psychosomatic health, self-healing, and illness as life-forces.

Five

MIND AND BODY LIVING TOGETHER: STAYING HEALTHY

Aging is the sum of all the stresses which have acted upon the body during a life span.   *[Selye, 1970, pp. 669-70]*

Legend has it that Gordius, king of ancient Phrygia, tied a knot which only the future ruler of Asia would be able to untie. Alexander the Great came along and undid the knot by cutting the rope with his sword. The term "Gordian knot" has thus come to mean an intricate problem that is insoluble in its own terms: The interrelationships between the human mind, personality, body, and environment are often referred to as an extraordinarily complex "Gordian knot," interwoven in ways that seem beyond unraveling.

For centuries, people have noticed that psychological conditions seem to be associated with illness. Most of us know from personal experience that being upset can result in some kind of body disturbance, such as indigestion or a headache. Some physicians are impressed by the influence of the psyche on susceptibility to physical disease. For example, several physicians accurately predicted that when Richard Nixon resigned as president in 1974, he would become ill.

At medical conventions these days, physicians are often admonished to treat the "whole patient." They are told to remember the psychosocial side—problems with the spouse, the job situation, and so on. Unfortunately, this advice is not often followed.

Nor is the unity of mind and body a concept universally endorsed by the medical profession. Conservative doctors view such ideas with mistrust, believing that psychosomatic facets of psychology are an untested science, which bears little relevance to real disease. These physicians tend to ignore the importance of stress. For example, a doctor sometimes treats a broken leg rather than a human being with a broken leg. A person in pain is scared and unhappy about being immobilized. He or she resents the uncomfortable cast, worries about being dependent, and frets about accomplishing the tasks of daily life. A person's life situation and personality, as well as the doctor's understanding of that person, greatly influence the healing process. The healing of a broken leg depends largely on blood supply and muscle tension; orthopedic surgeons, even those who are not known for their appreciation of psychology, admit that circulation and muscle tension are greatly influenced by emotions. Consequently, the viewpoint of this chapter is not unanimously accepted by medical personnel. But then few things are.

Hippocrates, Galen, and other early founders of modern medicine pointed out the intricate interactions between mind and body. So the problem of understanding mental/physical interaction has been with us for a long time. And it seems that each generation has to re-explore the relationship between mind and body, to reformulate it in new terms. In our century, psychology, biofeedback, animal experiments, the concepts of stress and personality types, and the study of people in changing environments have all sharpened our sword for cutting the Gordian knot of mind/body relationship.

A change in lifestyle and its effect on personality can illustrate the important relationship between psychological stress and health. For example, a study was made of Japanese men who moved to the United States. Despite the fact that both countries are industrialized, Japan has one of the lowest rates of heart disease in the world and the United States has one of the highest. The American death rate from heart disease is seven times higher than in Japan.

A University of California study (*Science News,* August 1975, p. 216) followed four thousand Japanese immigrants to the United States over a ten-year period. Three patterns of assimilation emerged. Those Japanese Americans who became totally Westernized, plunging into the frantic lifestyle of their new country, showed a heart disease rate five times higher than those who clung to their traditional Oriental values. Those who became Westernized but retained some links with their old culture showed a heart disease rate two and a half times higher than those who continued to follow traditional lifestyles. The third group, who maintained their cultural values, showed the same low incidence of heart disease as men in Japan.

Though the importance of such heart disease factors as smoking, exercise, cholesterol, heredity, blood pressure, diet, and weight is generally beyond dispute, they still provide only an incomplete estimate. Evidence strongly suggests that emotional stress, operating through the central nervous system, is also a major factor in heart disease. Most of the Japanese–American immigrants in the study did not significantly change their diet. The major change was in their lifestyles and in the stress they lived with.

The general cultural traits of being competitive, aggressive, and impatient were found in the Japanese who had high rates of heart disease. These traits were seldom seen in the

Japanese men who had low incidence of heart disease. The traditional Japanese culture has built-in buffers to stress that Americans lack. For example, their society is more stable and less mobile, with life structured around closely knit family groups. A vocational place in society is determined when a Japanese child is young. The traditional Japanese also observe a strict set of customs to guide their behavior, with emphasis on the groups' needs rather than on the individual.

Thus our style of life, social environment, personality, emotions, genetic predispositions, and external toxic agents all influence our health. Two kinds of evidence point to this conclusion: (1) findings on what happens to people who are exposed to psychologically stressful events and changes, and (2) patterns of personality and vulnerability to disease.

THE CONCEPT OF STRESS

Stress means pressure, tension, or strain, in response to certain events or circumstances. Stress can also be defined, according to Selye (1974), as the rate at which we live at any one moment.

While stress has long been recognized, the medical implications and understanding of the mechanisms are relatively new. Only forty years ago, Hans Selye correlated stress and health.

Today, we're surrounded by articles, books, and even commercials about stress. To say that we live under terrible stress in our modern era is simply stating the obvious. Stress can be induced by driving in heavy traffic or being in a crowd, or it can manifest itself in a poor relationship with your boss.

Unfortunately, the same word is used to describe both the event and the reaction, a blurring of distinction that causes confusion. The event itself is *not* stress; the stress is *your* reaction. Your personality type determines the degree of strain you experience. We are therefore victims not only of industrialization, but of our own reactions to its frantic pace.

Stress has positive aspects. For one thing, it helps us fight off danger or escape it. If you're crossing the street, for example, and a car is coming at you, you jump out of the way. Your body exhibits the effects of increased adrenalin flow, a quicker heartbeat, and higher blood pressure in response to the danger —all of which makes for fast reactions and the availability of physical strength. When you are ill, your body may also mobilize to fight off the stress of disease by raising your temperature, increasing your pulse rate, and releasing extra white blood cells into your bloodstream. Stress also often assumes challenging forms that stimulate and pleasurably intensify living. Without stress, life could grow boring, and boredom itself is a major stress factor.

We vary, on an individual basis, as to the kinds and amounts of pressure we can take. What is stress to one person may be stimulation to another. There is no one single description of what produces stress, since the same potential stress factor will produce dissimilar reactions in different individuals. Some people thrive when they have a lot of things to do, growing restless when there aren't enough demands and challenges. Other people are happiest when they are doing very little. How we react to stress depends on a number of things, such as personality, previous experiences, and the value we put on the activity.

Life represents growth and change. However, major changes cause stress in almost everybody. Any change in our life, even if desirable and pleasurable, necessitates some degree of disequilibrium and consequent adjustment. A barrage of changes occurring at once, over a short period of time, can be overwhelming; the immune system may weaken and sicken (Levine, 1971, p. 2).

There is an optimal level of stress for each individual; beyond that, resistance to illness diminishes. Dr. Thomas Holmes and Dr. Richard Rahe (1967) devised a scale of stressful life events to trace the relationship between psychological stress and disease susceptibility. The test is a list of forty-three common changes and events occurring in life that function as precursors of major illness. Holmes and Rahe began the chart by placing an arbitrary value of fifty "points worth of stress" on the change caused by getting married. They then had thousands of people of different ages, backgrounds, and social classes rank the stress of other changes in relation to the fifty-point stress of a marriage.

For an indication of your personal stress–illness susceptibility, try taking the test shown in Figure 5–1. Check the life events that have happened to you within the past two years. If the event happened more than two years ago but you still think about it a lot and it still bothers you, then check that item too. By the same token, if you feel sure that an event has caused little psychological stress, then reduce the points allocated for it. In doing this, remember that change in itself is usually stressful even if it is a happy change, such as getting married or buying a new home; remember also that *all change involves ambivalence and conflict,* even when pleasure or satisfaction is dominant. A new home means having to move, being responsible for repairs and maintenance, and making a financial commitment. Christmas is another example of a happy time, but it can also be stressful because of the demands of entertaining, buying the "right" gifts, and so on. Of course, not all change is bad. In fact—as we will explore later in this chapter—the person in poor health probably *needs* some life changes.

Those people who score a high total of life-change points are most likely to become ill. For example, heading the list of stressful life events is the death of a spouse. Women who have recently been widowed are much more likely to become ill or to die than others in the same age group (Parkes, 1972). For widowers, the death rate is 40 percent higher than normal during the six months following the death of their wives (Rahe & Lind, 1971, p. 19).

If you score over 300 points on this test, the odds are extremely high that you are over-stressed; and a good chance exists that you will respond with some kind of major sickness within the year. If you score less than 150 points, then your

Rank	Event	Average Points	Write Number of Points That Apply to You
1.	Death of spouse	100	_____
2.	Divorce	73	_____
3.	Marital separation	65	_____
4.	Jail term	63	_____
5.	Death of close family member	63	_____
6.	Personal injury or illness	53	_____
7.	Marriage	50	_____
8.	Fired at work	47	_____
9.	Marital reconciliation	45	_____
10.	Retirement	45	_____
11.	Change in health of family member	44	_____
12.	Pregnancy	40	_____
13.	Sex difficulties	39	_____
14.	Gain of new family member	39	_____
15.	Business readjustment	39	_____
16.	Change in financial state	38	_____
17.	Death of close friend	37	_____
18.	Change to different line of work	36	_____
19.	Change in number of arguments with spouse	35	_____
*20.	Mortgage over $10,000	31	_____
21.	Foreclosure of mortgage or loan	30	_____
22.	Change in responsibilities at work	29	_____
23.	Son or daughter leaving home	29	_____
24.	Trouble with in-laws	29	_____
25.	Outstanding personal achievement	28	_____
26.	Spouse begin or stop work	26	_____
27.	Begin or end school	26	_____
28.	Change in living conditions	25	_____
29.	Revision of personal habits	24	_____
30.	Trouble with boss	23	_____
31.	Change in work hours or conditions	20	_____
32.	Change in residence	20	_____
33.	Change in schools	20	_____
34.	Change in recreation	19	_____
35.	Change in church activities	19	_____
36.	Change in social activities	18	_____
*37.	Mortgage or loan less than $10,000	17	_____
38.	Change in sleeping habits	17	_____
39.	Change in number of family get-togethers	15	_____
40.	Change in eating habits	15	_____
41.	Vacation	13	_____
42.	Christmas	12	_____
43.	Minor violations of the law	11	_____

Total Points of Those Items That Apply to You _____

*Given inflation, we suggest you increase this to $30,000.

Figure 5–1. Life Events: The Stress of Adjusting to Change Chart. Reprinted with permission from *Journal of Psychosomatic Research,* Vol. 2, pp, 213–218, Holmes and Rahe, "The Social Readjustment Rating Scale," 1967, Pergamon Press, Ltd.

chances for a continuing state of health are good. A score between 150 and 300 indicates a moderate risk of illness.

Note that the stress scale is completely nonenvironmental and nonpolitical. It does not rate the stress of living in smog, in the midst of noise, or in the middle of crowds. It doesn't suggest anything about the effects of the major social causes of stress. It neither measures the tremendous energy it takes to live in an environment of injustice, repression, and violence, nor tells the strain of witnessing the suffering of others.

The Holmes-Rahe stress chart scale points out that, if possible, we should avoid making too many radical and stressful changes in our life at any one time. For example, a woman who is widowed is often faced with contingent changes in finances and social relationships. In counseling widows, I commonly hear a woman say she wants to move to a new place and change her living conditions: "This place has too many memories of him." And I very often strongly advise against doing so immediately. Not only does moving usually indicate an attempt to escape from the necessary process of grieving, but it also adds to that woman's stress rating by another change and another adjustment.

Draining or uprooting events are not the only stress factor. Stress can also occur due to a lack of meaning in life, isolation from others, and sustained boredom. Boredom, commonly treated with a band-aid of valium, is an increasingly common modern malady. As life expectancy and our expectations of quality-of-living increase, so does our vulnerability to boredom. For those who have decided that they must live their lives fully, "semi-full" can be deadly boring! Boredom can happen when the phone never stops ringing—or when it never rings at all. Or it may be a state of mind in which every day seems to mimic the previous day. In fact, boredom is one of the inescapable pains of living, and trying to escape that pain can create tremendous stress.

The meta-message of the Holmes stress chart, therefore, should not be interpreted to be, "Don't allow changes in your life." Though life's changes imply a degree of disequilibrium and adjustment, they cause stress only in relation to how we regard the activity or change. "Orgasm and running from a pursesnatcher both make the heart race, but the former produces less stress than the latter [Keen, 1976, personal letter]."

Stress is the wear and tear of everyday life; it's part of everything we do. We can't avoid it. Nor would we want to avoid stress, because the total absence of stress is death.

> The idea is not to try to avoid stress, but to make sure we live with *beneficial stress*—that is, feelings of pleasure, fulfillment, satisfaction. If we feel worthy and loved, we are less likely to develop the diseases that we now know are related to harmful stress or distress.   *[Selye, 1974, p. 96]*

What part does stress play in how we age? Selye (1970) believes that aging is the sum of all the stresses that have acted upon the body during a life span. Do we age the way a tree grows rings!? Perhaps so. Probably no other area of scientific inquiry abounds with so many untested theories as the biology of aging (Hayflick, 1975, p. 42); we have only begun to scratch the surface of knowledge.

But on the basis of recent research, we can make several observations about aging and stress. Aging as a process leads to increasing vulnerability to disease, partly because of stress resulting from many life changes, such as widowhood, friendship losses, financial losses, status losses, and retirement.

Yet longevity itself brings inevitable losses. And we are not taught in our society how to grieve and then "let go" upon the death of those we love. We need to be able to say good-bye to old joys and be open to creating new ones. An essential part of aging is learning to react to change with flexibility and acceptance.

Perhaps one of the greatest psychological losses in aging is the loss of hope that life will get better. "The failure of man to realize many of his existential life goals, is responsible for a majority of his health disturbances [Aakster, 1974, p. 77]." The stress of frustration often produces disease (Selye, 1974, p. 78).

Becoming older in our culture certainly entails frustrations and disappointments. We treat old people as useless, nonproductive failures. If an older person accepts and internalizes these values, it is no wonder he or she becomes ill.

People who have a reason for living most likely live longer and better. Metropolitan Life Insurance Company (1974), in a study of 1,078 corporate executives over a sixteen-year period, found evidence to contradict the popular opinion that business executives suffer from heart disease, ulcers, hypertension, and early death. These men show a mortality rate 37 percent *lower* than the general population. Why do executives live so long? Metropolitan explains that they are emotionally and physically fit for coping with stressful situations. They are able to harness tensions for productive use, deriving from their work satisfaction as well as recognition and high social status. "Successful activity, no matter how intense, leaves you with comparatively few scars; it causes stress but little if any distress [Selye, 1974, p. 96]." In situations when the business failed or the executives were retired, their health deteriorated accordingly.

In our culture, society exerts a "stressor role" by imposing on older people unreal and unnecessary youth standards. The banner reads, "Old is ugly/Young is beautiful!"

REDUCING STRESS

Centenarians from many geographic locations throughout the world were asked, "To what do you attribute your long and healthy life? [Leaf, 1973]." The local alcoholic beverage was most often credited for their healthy aging (p. 49)! On a scientific level, moderate consumption of alcohol could be conceived as an aid to the digestive system. However, if we accept these statements as anything but naive or superficial, the alcoholic beverage could simply represent relaxation; the alcohol *per se* is not the cause of longevity, but rather its ability to relax tensions. These centenarians, in other words, knew how to relax.

None of us can avoid stress entirely, but we can do certain things to ease the effects of unproductive stress. In other words, most of us have to learn how to relax.

Just as stress is increasingly identified as the root of the modern malaise, so relaxation through meditation is now seen as a major antidote. Blood pressure can be lowered with relaxation techniques (Redmond, 1974); arthritis and many other painful conditions respond also. Also, people who meditate or know how to relax recover rapidly from stress; meditators can withstand more life changes with less illness than other people (Goleman, 1976, p. 82).

Dr. Herbert Benson, of Harvard Medical School, in studying the physiological responses to meditation, found the *relaxation response* to be the opposite of the *stress syndrome.* Wallace and Benson (1972) discovered that, with relaxation, the following changes typically occur:

- lower metabolic rate,
- reduced oxygen consumption,
- decreased heart and respiration rates,
- greater resistance of the skin to mild electric current (related to the amount of tension present), and
- changes in brain wave patterns.

Why does the body respond in these ways during relaxation? One reason seems to be basic to most kinds of relaxation: that is, focusing on and doing one thing at a time. The signals to our bodies are simpler and more coherent during relaxation than at most other times. The other signals in the course of a day are extremely complex. For instance, if I am talking to you, I am not only speaking but I am also thinking about where the conversation is going, what has already been said, how I feel about the subject, what I am noticing about you, what your reactions are, what the time is, and so on. In the background of my thoughts are memories of the earlier parts of the day and plans for the rest of today. In addition, I am conscious of my fatigue level and I wish it were lunchtime. My body is receiving signals regarding each of these general mental states.

In relaxation we are in or moving toward the state of handling a single set of signals at a time. Research shows that the effect of this on our physiology is positive. Tension and anxiety are reduced.

Meditation, of course, isn't the only way to relax or to reduce stress; many physical means, such as sensory awareness, Tai Chi, athletics, dancing, and simple chores like housework, do as well. The objective is to do one pleasurable, relaxing activity as completely and as fully as possible (LeShan, 1974, p. 42).

Immersing ourselves in any relaxing activity feels good. Relaxation is one of life's joys (although, to some people, it may seem like a dull duty). The feelings accompanying the relaxation response are positive: Most people feel more energy, well-being, or a sense of calmness. If you don't have a positive reaction, then perhaps that type of relaxation or meditation isn't the right one for you. Try different ones. Find what feels most natural for you as an individual.

AGING AND THE DISEASE OF CANCER

If heart disease, stroke, and cancer were eliminated, the American public could expect approximately twenty years of additional life (Hayflick, 1975, p. 36). Though heart disease is the number one killer, cancer is still the dreaded disease. More than 675,000 persons in the United States will discover this year that they have some form of cancer: Over half will die from it (*Science News,* January 1976).

Who gets cancer and why? And why does one person develop heart disease, another cancer, and still another remains healthy?

Originally, cancer was thought to be contagious—it seemed

to run in families. Other members of a cancer patient's family contracted the same disease so often that physicians thought it was a viral disease that simply spread. Then, the theory of cancer susceptibility was supplanted by a theory of genetic vulnerability, in which cancer was thought to be an inherited biological weakness. Now some health professionals believe cancer to be a psychologically related disease.

Psychosomatic, a term describing the interaction of the *psyche* (mind) and *soma* (body), is a volatile word even when associated with illnesses such as ulcers, hypertension, and rheumatoid arthritis. Now, in the heat of controversy, these individuals are seriously considering the idea that psychological factors may be involved in the development of cancer and in its occasional remission.

Carl Simonton, M.D., a radiation therapist and cancer specialist, is convinced that one's state of mind has to do with the development of cancer. "The mind, the emotions and the attitude of a patient play a role in both the development of a disease, cancer included, and the response that a patient has to any form of treatment [Bolen, 1973, p. 19]."

Do we know enough to say that cancer can be psychologically induced? Simonton says yes. He points out that according to current immunological theory, "The cancer cell is a weak and vacillating cell, most often defeated by the body's own immune mechanism. The fact is that all of us have had cancer many times. Without knowing it, the white blood cells of our immune mechanisms have defeated the weaker cancer cells [Elwell, 1975, p. 42]." What is unusual in cancer is not that malignant cells arise, but that for some reason the body allows these cells to grow, when it normally and routinely destroys them.

Psychological factors and environmental stresses can influence the immunological response. For example, a strain of mice carrying a cancer virus developed cancers 92 percent of the time when they were exposed to a stressful environment; similarly infected mice who were protected from such stress developed cancer only 7 *percent* of the time (*Science News,* March 1975, p. 182)! The study of the effects of stress, and the corresponding development of cancer in animals, indicates that the physiological effects of stress lead to an impairment of the defense system and increased susceptibility to cancer.

Dr. Simonton believes that cancer patients not only allow their disease to come into being, but that they also have the power to heal themselves (Elwell, 1975, p. 41). He utilizes medical treatment of the body with the full participation of the mind and encourages his patients to use self-healing techniques of visualization, relaxation, meditation, and biofeedback to mobilize healing. While the use of relaxation and mental imagery to cure cancer is still not established, the claims of Simonton and others like him can no longer be ignored.

SELF-HEALING

Our thoughts and feelings can cause us to become physically ill . . . and they can heal us when we become ill. Visualization for self-healing is an ancient curing art that is being rediscovered. Dr. Mike Samuels goes into this subject in depth in his excellent book, *Seeing with the Mind's Eye* (1975).

Self-healing works by combining meditation (focused concentration) with mental pictures (visualization). The visualizations are of the illness either in the process of healing or completely healed and in a state of health.

In 1970 the Menninger Foundation conducted a series of studies on Swami Rama, a yogi. Rama uses visualization with his meditations to control his body functioning. The Menninger Foundation found that Rama could:

> . . . cause two areas a couple inches apart on the palm of his right hand to gradually change temperature in opposite directions until there showed a temperature difference of ten degrees F. The left side of his palm looked as if it had been slapped with a ruler, it was rosy red. The right side of his hand had turned ashen gray.
>
> *[Samuels & Samuels, 1975, p. 222]*

Swami Rama did this by mentally visualizing the body change he wanted: He pictured one part of his palm submerged in ice water and the other part in burning coals. Rama is also able to raise his heart rate from seventy beats per minute to three hundred by visualization.

One of Dr. Simonton's patients describes a visualization he used:

> I'd begin to visualize my cancer—as I saw it in my mind's eye. I'd make a game of it. The cancer would be a snake, a wolverine or some vicious animal. The cure, white husky dogs by the millions. It would be a confrontation of good and evil. I'd envision the dogs grabbing the cancer and shaking it, ripping it to shreds. The forces of good would win. The cancer would shrink—from a big snake to a little snake—and then disappear. Then the white army of dogs would lick up the residue and clean my abdominal cavity until it was spotless.　　　　　　　　　*[Samuels & Samuels, 1975, p. 227]*

The cancer patient did this type of self-healing three times a day for ten to fifteen minute intervals. After two months, the patient had no cancer left in his body (p. 227).

Self-healing through autogenetic therapy is meditative visualization of a desirable state of health. Schultz and Luthe (cited in Samuels & Samuels, 1975) have written a seven-volume work on how autogenetic therapy works, in which they cite over twenty-four hundred studies of its successful application to disease. It has been successfully used to treat a number of illnesses: heart attacks, angina, ulcers, gastritis, gallbladder attacks, hemorrhoids, high blood pressure, headaches, asthma, diabetes, thyroid disease, arthritis, and back pain.

In autogenetics, programmed meditation is used by a therapist. The patient is told to sit or lie comfortably and to imagine physical states or conditions as suggested by the therapist. For instance, a person is directed to tell himself, "My arms are heavy," and to concentrate on producing this body sensation, as a way of relaxing. Other messages might be, "My forehead is cool" or "My heartbeat is calm and regular."

Self-regulation of health is a potential area of medicine which is largely unexplored. It is now generally medically accepted, however, that it is possible for a patient to exert some control over cardiac functions (Blanchard & Young, 1973) and blood pressure (Redmond, 1974). A number of other conditions, including cancer, may also be psychologically influenced in ways that we need to examine in greater depth.

BIOFEEDBACK

Until recently, reports about the remarkable ability of yogis to control specific bodily functions were not given much credence, since much of our physical functioning—especially the autonomic nervous system—was assumed to be beyond conscious control. Traditionally, many body functions have been presumed involuntary.

Recent studies show that control over the autonomic nervous system can be learned by paying attention to very subtle internal signals. The pioneering studies by Miller and Dicara revealed that animals could learn to alter their blood flow, blood pressure, stomach acidity, and brain wave patterns in response to reward (Miller, 1969). The human correlative of these laboratory animal experiments has been the birth of biofeedback.

Biofeedback is a technique that tells people what is happening inside their bodies, by employing instruments that elicit visual or auditory signals. The feedback is specific and continues from moment to moment (Jonas, 1973, p. 27). For instance, a person is attached to an apparatus that graphically and continuously shows his or her muscle tension; in this way, a person can lower muscle tension by the use of biofeedback. The electronic biofeedback system provides the person with information about the activity of internal organs; apparently, the individual is then capable of consciously regulating to some extent the specific body functioning.

Indications are that biofeedback may have important medical applications for the elderly and for some diseases. "As a behavioral intervention to affect physiological decline in the elderly, biofeedback has great potential. With this technique we may be able to demonstrate that there is residual capacity in the older (or diseased) organism which we would have never believed existed [Woodruff, 1975b, p. 189]." It has been used to reduce hypertension, to treat migraine headaches, and to counter some forms of epilepsy.

It may also be a help to stroke patients recovering from muscle paralysis (*Human Behavior,* 1976). Biofeedback has been used as an electronic mirror that alerts the stroke patient to the slightest muscle activity via a buzzer or a red light. For example, a common stroke-induced condition is known as "footdrop"—the inability to control the dorsal muscle which keeps the foot from dragging. Using a biofeedback device to signal muscle activity in the ankle, the stroke patient sees the muscle is active and is able to learn to increase the activity. After using biofeedback, many patients learn the process so well that they have no further need for biofeedback reinforcement. They are able to work for full muscle recovery on their own.

Scientific research in aging has always looked for decline —for things that older people do less well than younger people. Rarely have we looked for what older people can do better. In biofeedback older people have actually learned more quickly than younger people (Woodruff, 1975b, p. 194). "This was amazing, for there had been some speculation that it would not be possible to train the old people at all. But, on second thought, a person who has been living in his body for sixty-five years probably knows a lot more about it than one who has only been in it for twenty years [p. 194]." It may be that as we grow older and become more in tune with our bodies, we can develop better ways to maintain health and recover from illness.

"FAITH HEALING": THE POWER OF THE MIND

Medical science is moving beyond a simple cause-and-effect model of disease to a multifactorial picture. As we have said, the climate for disease is created by a number of elements, such as stress, personality type, virus, genetic background, and pollution. The factors that help to preserve health include psychological harmony, exercise, good diet, and a lucky genetic base. Healing occurs when you reduce the causes of disease and strengthen defenses. Clearly, the more variables you're able to identify and deal with in disease, the greater your chances for improved health. The concept of disease is useful only if it encourages us to look beyond the obvious. Likewise, the boundaries of healing must extend beyond the areas we have traditionally called "scientific."

Faith healing is becoming recognized as an acceptable practice by some health professionals. Although still seen as doubtful by the majority of physicians, even some medical doctors approve its utilization under specified circumstances.

Related to faith healing is the placebo, the phenomenon of curing through the psychological dynamic of believing one will get well, which in itself appears to be healing. The placebo effect, an extremely significant healing device, is so powerful that its unscientific elements have to be carefully isolated from true results in medical research. However, in doing so, we impose serious limits on the dimensions of healing. In Western medicine we have made a religion out of denying religion— that is, whatever is unconscious and pre-scientific. We have habitually bowed to statistics, white coats, and experts; we are only now beginning to look past them to the range of the possible.

In looking at less traditional modes of science, we need to balance skepticism and receptivity, to keep an open mind. Methodology, not subject matter, distinguishes science from the irrational or pseudo-scientific. Frazier (1976) points out that many critics of pre-scientific phenomena argue for professional elitism. They presume a superior attitude and can be even more irresponsible with facts and arguments than those they criticize.

Usually we resent being ill. Illness seems meaningless, a waste of time, energy, money, and health. Consequently, we adopt the attitude that illness is something imposed from the outside: It "attacks" us; we are powerless "victims." Once attacked, we believe that only a physician can cure us. The medical doctor then treats the symptoms but rarely searches into the personal meaning expressed through the illness.

For example, some of the employees at a tuberculosis sanitarium developed the disease themselves. The sick employees were compared to other employees also exposed to the disease who remained healthy. Traditional medicine might reflect on the fact that the bacillus were present in the sick employees and were causing tuberculosis, but it would not ask why the disease appeared only in some employees. What caused these persons to become hosts to the disease-causing bacillus? Why did some employees get the disease, while others remained healthy? Why did some persons have lowered bodily resistance, and others immunity? Usually the physicians simply diagnosed and began treatment with medication. The fact that high psychological stress is hypothesized to be antecedent to the disease would not, in all likelihood, be explored (Rahe *et al.,* 1964).

Physicians rarely take the time to help a patient explore what purpose a disease might be serving in his/her life. In most medical situations, the doctor takes the active role of enacting a procedure upon the sick person, who remains passive. The sick person, not viewing the illness as a signal with meaning, doesn't try to understand causes. Instead, the passive patient awaits improved health by "following doctor's orders," rather than by also actively seeking self-healing. Keen (1976) states that:

> . . . disease has replaced sin as the condition from which we must be saved. . . . The doctor becomes the patient's accomplice in creating the myth that he is an innocent victim of biological mechanisms. The physician, as enlightened priest of science, absolves the

sick from any moral responsibility for their illness. . . . By turning patients into passive consumers, objects to be repaired, voyeurs of their own treatment, the medical enterprise saps the will of people to suffer their own reality. It destroys our autonomous ability to cope with our own bodies and heal ourselves.   *[p. 73]*

Ease and dis-ease are expressions in the body of a total life situation. They are dependable indicators for choosing directions to determine how we feel. Our bodies are barometers of harmony and disharmony, and the many subtleties in between. If we apply medication to symptoms without examining what they indicate, we lose the opportunity to learn about ourselves. Ignoring the meaning of disease is to lose the message expressed.

When an illness has been long in developing, such as cancer or hypertension, it can seem overwhelming to face both the physical illness and the change barometer. If we accept responsibility for being sick, there's a tendency to feel guilty for what we have done to ourselves or to our families, or discouraged at our failure to create a harmonious life. Illness is a time when we must be kind and gentle with ourselves. It is an opportunity for growth, and, while growth is often triggered by pain, it is nourished by self-acceptance and love. To blame ourselves for illness is to intensify the dis-ease. Most of us impose far too many perfectionist standards upon ourselves as it is.

FINDING THE MEANING OF DISEASE

The Institute for the Study of Humanistic Medicine suggests questions to ask ourselves regarding the value and meaning of disease:

- Is there a message in the experiences of my illness?
- Am I attempting to "get healed" before I have a chance to see the larger picture?

- Could my illness be an attempt by my body to provide an interruption, to permit me to re-evaluate my life patterns and purpose?
- How can I make use of this illness as an avenue for personal development?
- How can this illness be used creatively in my life?
- What are the possible implications of this illness in terms of the values by which I am living?
- How can I improve my life situation, so that I'm more at ease with it?   *[Belknap et al., 1975]*

The Institute believes that contemplation of the meaning of illness must become a part of the treatment program between professionals and patients. If symptoms are erased without gaining insight, the individual is likely to go through life with unrecognized or unresolved stresses and self-alienation. Illness can then become a recurrent pattern, with a medicine cabinet full of temporary-relief therapies. With growing older, sickness and its manifestations can become progressively worse if the body's signals are ignored.

Staying on a life course that is creating disease may seem irrational, even self-destructive, when viewed abstractly. Despite signs of dis-ease, we like to leave things unchanged. However, if we choose this course, disharmony and stress will continue, so that, with aging, we are highly vulnerable to a breakdown in our immunity system and consequently to a major illness.

DISEASE IS NOT PART OF THE AGING PROCESS

Diseases occur more frequently with aging, although they are not an integral part of the aging process. Many diseases, including hypertension and cancer, may take ten to twenty years to develop obvious symptoms: *The illnesses of older people actually often start up during youth or the middle years.* For example, many American men already have internal symptoms of coronary heart disease in their early twenties, although the symptoms do not become evident until their fifties or sixties.

Older people recover from disease much more slowly than younger people. By way of evidence, the elderly have longer average stays in the hospital. But factors other than the power to recover lengthen this stay, for instance, unfavorable home situations and the hospital staff's lack of confidence in the patient's potential to rehabilitate. Rehabilitation of the older patient should begin at the onset of illness, and inactivity should be avoided.

> The fact is that an older person can recover from an acute illness almost as rapidly as a younger person, assuming he is otherwise in good health and is normally motivated. Given a good blood supply and the proper state of nutrition, the older patient's tissues will heal well. *[USDHEW, 1966, p. 2]*

The body's reaction to disease often changes with aging. For example, temperature may rise only slightly in illnesses characterized by high fever in younger people. This body temperature response is thought to be due to the changes in metabolism discussed in the previous chapter. In general, older people manifest fewer and more subtle signs of illness than younger persons. Many older people also have greater pain tolerance. When mental changes occur in the elderly, such as disorientation and confusion, the first assumption should be a physical explanation. A diagnosis of senility (discussed in Chapter 2) should never be made until all other possible physical causes are eliminated.

POLLUTION

Pollutants in the air and water, chemicals in our food, noise in our surroundings, toxins in industrial waste products—all these can harm our health. Living without the many benefits of science is hard to imagine. However, living with them is getting harder. Especially since the end of World War II, we have seen a quantum leap in the invasion of our physical environment by harmful chemicals and pollution.

As we age, the toxic effects can accumulate. In addition to accumulative toxicity, older persons apparently have less effective liver-enzyme defenses against toxic chemicals than younger persons. Taking some precautions against pollution is therefore wise:

- avoid foods that contain additives and artificial colorings;
- wash produce that may have been sprayed;
- avoid unnecessary X-rays; and
- avoid smoking and avoid unventilated areas inhabited by smokers.

While reasonable precautions are in order, you need not become obsessed with "purity." Worrying about it can produce stress that might be more damaging than the pollutants themselves. For example, when I wake up in the morning I immediately think of brushing my teeth and having a cup of coffee. Now, for the pleasure of drinking coffee I may be courting cancer, ulcers, and heart disease. If I switch to drinking decaffinated coffee (and give up the sweet/bitter/lovely smell of "real" coffee), I could still worry about cancer, since chemicals are used in the decaffination process. Meanwhile, I go into the bathroom to brush my teeth. My toothpaste is composed of many chemicals and has toxic lead in its container, which dissolves into the toothpaste. My tap water is probably not pure either. If I choose to worry about all this, I've eliminated my morning pleasures and a happy beginning to a new day—which we consider more damaging than the toxic chemicals.

While we have fairly conclusive evidence about the harmful effects of smoking, other toxic penalties are less clear. *Our immunity is complex and individualized.* Eliminate as much toxic pollution as possible, taking good care of yourself; at the same time enjoy your small, personal pleasures, even if they are not entirely pure.

For many years we accepted the extreme view that people are the passive "victims" of disease. In advocating that we take responsibility for our illnesses and find meaning in the experience of sickness, it is important to understand that not all health problems—or perhaps not even most—arise from psychosocial causes. Emotions are involved in any disease; however, there is not always a cause-and-effect relationship between an emotion and a pathology. Multiple causes are possible for any single illness, including genetic predisposition, stress, noxious agents (for example, virus, injury), and accidental factors. Accidents are a reality. Similarly, when exposed to a virus, such as influenza, a person is very likely to contract the disease, regardless of psychosocial factors.

Westerners tend to think dualistically about human functions, splitting things into mental and physical categories. "Psychosomatic" was originally coined to express the fact that mind and body are interacting processes rather than separate entities. The term has come to connote that an illness is "all in the head," imaginary, a sign of malingering or of defective character. For this reason the term "psychophysiological" is replacing the word "psychosomatic." For example, an ulcer is certainly not imaginary, whether it is psychosomatic or not. An ulcer is a real lesion in the stomach lining. And the person who is sick is usually quite the opposite of a malingerer. In fact, ulcers, like heart disease, are often due to the stress of working too hard; and cancer may be due to a weakened immunity because of taking difficult emotions out on one's self.

Assuming psychodynamics is accepted as a working hypothesis in medicine, one of the dangers is that, when a disease persists, the patient might be accused of "not trying hard enough" to heal, to relax, to meditate, or whatever. Understandably, disease will prevail from time to time. "Being sick and suffering are inevitable human experiences [Keen, 1976, p. 73]." Sometimes we can do no more than accept the reality of sickness with gracefulness and flexibility.

Successful aging means accepting not only inevitable death but also probable illness and some resultant physical deterioration. If we have learned how to conserve our energy, to "let go" of what we must, to be open to new experiences, and to be flexible in accepting new directions, then aging will continue to offer pleasures in living. The search for perfect health and perpetual youth is one of the worst diseases of aging in America.

Health professionals who provide services to older people must also understand that caring for a patient sometimes means accepting illness. Health professionals are usually trained to *combat* sickness, rather than to accept it. For many young physicians, the most frustrating and upsetting professional experience is not the patient's failure to pay the bill, but the patient's failure to recover completely. The health professional's expectations for health must be neither unrealistically high nor so low as to encourage unnecessary deterioration.

Of course, no health guarantee or future insurance exists for any of us. Hopefully, rather than becoming chronically absorbed in our health symptoms as we grow older, we will have the audacity to solve our human dilemma by taking action in defense of the pleasure of living. We can age without abdicating the full experience of living.

> The tragedy of life is not what men suffer but rather what they miss.
> *[Thomas Carlyle]*

In this respect, "Western" enculturation differs from the Eastern way. Eastern philosophy encourages the continuing development of the inner self through introspection. Wisdom and spirituality are considered the highest virtues for the aged. For some people this goal may represent developmental fulfillment, but for others it is a severely limited modality. Protect yourself from such patent prescriptions. Practice your own version of experience. Aging can be a time to express your bold demands for enhanced personal freedom, uninhibited sensuality, the joy of earned idleness, and euphoric sensations. As you grow older, you do not need perfect health to find excitement, or to satisfy your erotic inclinations.

Older people have been particularly vulnerable to the morality of abstention from pleasure. For one thing, their energy is admittedly decreased. Beyond that reason, however, a rigid social attitude limits them to the meditative virtues and to acting "dignified." In Chapter 7 we maintain that human dignity does not reside in renouncing the sweet pleasures of life, but rather in satisfying the need to explore life courageously—in applying as many of our individual capacities as possible. An obsession with purity—whether it be health, work, or wisdom—can make us sick if it forbids us the joys of life. Living in our modern world takes the "guts" to break away from traditional modes of stressful living and behavioral attitudes; it takes an "open mind" to consider seriously some of the more intuitive, personal health approaches, such as those discussed in this chapter. Personal liberation from unhealthy traditions can be the reward that comes with aging.

DEVELOPMENTAL TASKS
OF AGING

As you age, you have certain things to do, tasks to perform. These *developmental tasks* of aging are determined by biological and social realities and require significant adjustments. Although aging is unique for each individual, certain changes in life are common enough to cut across ethnic and socioeconomic variables. You must successfully cope with each specific task in order to continue your personal development. Aging forces you to deal with the discontinuity of change. The resolutions may be gains, losses, or a combination of both.

The following situations are part of growing older in most of the industrialized, critical issues that must be confronted:

- changes in energy and health;
- decreased sensorium; changes in sexuality and sensuousness; reduced psychomotor effectiveness;

- loss of social roles, changes in status, retirement, and economics; loss of friends or spouse or peers; problems of identity, loneliness, boredom, and depression; and
- death and dying.

CHANGES IN ENERGY AND HEALTH

At any age, developing priorities for how we use our energy is important: In old age it is *vital.*

While normal aging is not itself a disease, more than two-thirds of older Americans have some chronic disability, although most such individuals function very well nonetheless and are only minimally affected. The most common chronic illnesses are arthritis, diabetes, deafness, and visual problems. Any disease—a drain on the system—can affect how much energy we have.

Physical disabilities and the time spent incapacitated, though dependent on the individual, are also correlated with socioeconomic level. For example, a man of seventy-five with an annual income of $15,000 or more averages twenty days a year of restricted activity due to poor health. A person of the same age with an income of under $5,000 a year averages thirty-one days a year of illness (Kimmel, 1974, pp. 359–360).

People commonly complain about loss of energy as they grow older. For this reason, older people are usually advised, "Conserve your energy." However, much of the exhaustion attributed to aging actually is due to depression. Depression can be caused partly by poor health or poverty, but it is also likely to be related to poor adjustment to losses and to a lack of preparation for aging.

The early years are the time to prepare for the later years. Those who live their lives well are preparing for a happy old age. Often middle age is so burdened with hard work and striving for accomplishment that you forget how to live and enjoy. You are then likely to enter old age chronically depressed, particularly if your life has been outer-directed, with relatively few inner resources.

Rather than conserve energy and thereby perpetuate depression, learn how to stimulate and generate your energy. Don't, for instance, fight what your body tells you. Some older people can go without sleeping for three days; others need eight or more hours of sleep a night. Older people tend also to sleep less deeply; they wake up during the night, often several times, and they are unable to sleep late in the morning. On the other hand, they normally take catnaps during the day. Unfortunately, since they are typically told in this culture that a "good night's sleep is essential," they will toss and turn or resort to sleep medication. Trying to follow a preconceived schedule goes against their body-truth and results in a waste of energy.

When we're having a good time, we suddenly have much more energy and we need less sleep. A boring, tedious, uneventful, or over-scheduled, dutiful, doing-what-others-expect life is exhausting. More rest is required because of the strain of living through it all and not doing what we like.

Energy level is psychologically related to life satisfaction. Giving yourself permission to experience pleasure and to eliminate unpleasant expenditures of time often results in a release of energy.

> Time (and personal energy) is the coin of your life. It is the only coin you have. Be careful lest someone else spend it for you.
>
> *[Carl Sandburg]*

The worst that should happen to you as you age is that your activities might be quantitatively reduced . . . while gaining in quality. With aging, many people have less tolerance for doing things that they don't enjoy or things that they feel are a waste of their time and energy. Some of us expect that growing older means gaining personal time and freedom: It then becomes increasingly difficult to continue work that may be unpleasant or undesirable—and draining.

Impaired health or physical incapacity may require letting

go of some activities that you found pleasurable and valuable in the past. However, studies show that older people tend to maintain the same relative levels and types of activities in their later years as they had during younger ages (Palmore and Manton, 1973). Recent longitudinal evidence tends to question the extent of an age-related reduction of energy: They contradict the findings of the older cross-sectional surveys (and the common assumption) that most people become less energetic and active because of aging (Palmore & Manton, 1973). For example, people who enjoy walking will continue to do so but may reduce their speed; or they reduce the steepness of their ski runs, or the vigor of their tennis, and so on. Although aging may call for appropriate reductions of energy, especially in competition sports, the lifestyle persists.

The point is to maintain a balance between realistic caution and stalwartness. Often an activity can be modified rather than given up. Too frequently, people stop pleasurable activities so they will have enough energy for "what needs to be done." This tendency can spiral into decreasing energy.

Conversely, doing what pleases you can be invigorating. In interviews with energetic older people, they all commented that sometimes they wake up in the morning feeling pain, such as from arthritis, which can be tiring. However, they say that with chronic pain or tiredness they either "ignore it" or "tell it to go away," because "I won't let it get me down." They also comment that several hours later (if they stop to think about it), they're startled to realize how energetic and well they feel: ". . . doing things you like makes the difference."

Research indicates that there is no change in "life force" that is necessarily a part of aging (Cameron, 1975). Our interests, energy, moods, intensity of affect, and attitudes are not necessarily changed by growing older unless health factors intervene. Pleasure nourishes the "life force," and any pleasurable activity needs to be carefully assessed before being discarded. Positive energy begets more of the same. Most of us have a far greater capacity for energy than we use.

LOSSES THROUGH RETIREMENT

Our socialization process does not prepare us for living with losses. Learning to do so is one of the major developmental tasks of aging. One such loss is a change in work status. Achievement, money. success, and power are the usual criteria upon which people anchor their identity. In our society, your personal value often depends on what you do. One of the first questions that many people ask, when meeting someone new, is "What do you do?" The older retired person must adjust to the fact that his or her inner answers are changing.

Work is usually double-edged. It is an obligation with certain drudgeries; it is also a steadying element that gives a person a place in society and a definition of existence. Retirement reflects this ambivalence. For most people, a job not only provides the necessities of life, it is the source of social standing, self-respect, worth, and meaning. Freud saw work as one of the vital factors of a good life. Tampering with the work role can consequently profoundly affect an older person.

However, those who are prepared for retirement and expect a positive experience are very likely to have it; expectations about retirement become another self-fulfilling prophecy (Glamser, 1976).

Retirement can never be regarded as a single process. It is an event, a social definition, a new status, an economic situation, and a psychological adjustment. Retirement means, for some people, a psychological disaster of suddenly being thrown from action into inaction. Most seriously it can also be a financial disaster. Retirement has the advantage of leisure. The disadvantage is that leisure can make a person feel useless, nonproductive, and bored.

Adaptation to retirement would be easier if our society changed its traditions and attitudes toward leisure and also redefined "productivity." Certainly, a paycheck is not the only criterion of worthwhile time expenditure.

RETIREMENT: TO OR FROM LIFE?

Some of the specific advantages in retiring can be: freedom from deadlines and boring day-to-day responsibilities; freedom from competitiveness and its stresses; freedom from supervision and accountability to a boss. Retirement offers the opportunity to be yourself, freed from social demands. You can choose your own pace and determine your own time schedule; you can set your own goals. Retirement is a release from a network of external demands. •

Thus, retirement offers both an end and a beginning, both a difficult change and new opportunity. To live a satisfying life relatively free from familiar social roles can be a staggering challenge. It can also be a straitjacket for those who have made work a way of life and a justification for existence. Today the middle-class and the professional persons, afflicted with a chronic case of the work ethic, have the most difficulty adjusting to retirement (Maddox, 1970).

> The most important point may well be to teach people how to cope with free time, not by filling up free time with a string of compulsively carried out activities, but by developing attitudes which will permit a person to be with himself, perhaps by himself, in a truly leisurely manner. As we have been taught to work, not just by acquiring certain skills, but by acquiring the "right" work attitude, so perhaps must we now learn how to leisure.
>
> *[Neulinger & Raps, 1972, p. 206]*

Retirement is such a complex event that it even produces contradictory research findings (Goudy, Powers & Keith, 1975). One study concluded that no relationship exists between the commitment to work and the attitude toward retirement (Glamser, 1976). Another study found the exact opposite: How much we enjoy our jobs influences how we will feel about retirement (Fillenbaum, 1971).

Though research has been unsuccessful in discerning how

a person will react to retirement, it has shed light on what happens after retirement. About three out of ten retired men in the United States say that they enjoy *nothing* about their retirement (Shanas, 1970, p. 20). The rest of the retired men report "something about their retirement that they like," such as having free time and the opportunity to do the things they want (Shanas, p. 20). Most men say that they miss their work.

For almost half of them, the money is what they miss most. The sharp reduction in income is probably the most difficult part of the adjustment—most certainly a realistic concern. The majority of retired people have a severe drop in income. The average reduction is 50 percent below pre-retirement levels (Kimmel, 1974). In many instances the trauma of retirement is due to the fear of poverty.

Our culture puts the older retired person in a double bind. The popular image of successful aging is the person who stays actively involved, acts young, dresses well, and has high morale. But the financial resources necessary for this role are largely unavailable to older people because of mandatory retirement and the resulting poverty. It is, of course, a myth that older people have no desires beyond a warm rocking chair and sufficient food. The more "alive" an older person is, the more frustrating poverty can be (Tissue, 1971–72).

Many pleasures, such as travel, must be purchased. In our culture, people have been taught to consume pleasures rather than to generate them. Dr. Scitovsky, professor of economics at Stanford University, made a ten-year study comparing Americans' and Europeans' ability to enjoy leisure. He found that Europeans enjoy leisure more, need less money for their pleasures, and take more vacations. "The Europeans enjoy simpler things—often they use a vacation for a walking tour, camping out at night. That's a sharp contrast to the American way of seeing how many miles can be driven in an air-conditioned auto between one luxury motel and another [Martin, 1976]." Europeans are much more enthusiastic about hobbies, such as photography, gardening, and the like. And they hurry less, taking a longer time for such basic pleasures. For example, the American allots an average of seventy minutes a day for meals; the European spends almost a half-hour *more* each day in enjoyment of food (Martin, 1976).

How a person feels about poverty depends on the individual's goals. Many people, for example, deliberately choose a lifestyle of nonmaterialism. Others are unhappy with an income of $50,000 per year.

However, the consensus of gerontology research is that the older person who is poor is more likely to be unhappy (Riley & Foner, 1968). While many creative, energetic older people live happy lives on very little money, doing so is difficult in our society; a well-developed capacity for finding simple pleasures is certainly the first prerequisite for getting by on limited means.

ADJUSTMENT TO RETIREMENT

A survey by Tissue (1971–72) found that the most bothersome problems for older, retired people were:

- money (64 percent)
- nostalgia for a job (49 percent)
- missing one's family (48 percent)
- boredom (37 percent)
- transportation (32 percent)
- health (31 percent)
- loneliness (29 percent)
- uselessness (26 percent)
- housing (23 percent)
- not enough to do (16 percent)

Basically, retirement must be an adjustment to "being" as well as to "doing." Retirement is very much like having major surgery: Immediately after the operation, many people are euphoric—they've weathered a major event, survived. They are on the other side. Similarly, the first couple of months of retirement are spent doing chores and enthusiastically catching up on things left undone over the busy preceding years. But after a while, boredom often seeps in.

> The tragedy is that most of us are unprepared for old age. We know a great deal about what to do with things, even what to do with people; we hardly know what to do with ourselves. We know how to act in public; we do not know what to do in privacy. Old age involves the problem of what to do with privacy.
>
> *[Cooley & Cooley, 1972, p. 246]*

For many people, the only privacy they have ever sought was in the management of bodily functions. Sometimes the bathroom is the only room in a house secure from intrusion.

Indicative of our low premium on privacy and solitude is a 1975 survey on "What Makes You Happy?" published by *Psychology Today*. The "Happiness Survey," written by the Psychology Department of Columbia University, asked readers 123 intimate questions regarding what makes them happy. The questionnaire asked how much time they spent each day with people and doing various activities, but *not a single question was asked about time spent or enjoyment derived from being alone*. (Freedman & Shaver, 1975).

"The empty life is filled with tears" (Japanese proverb). In our society, we live up to that saying. We aren't encouraged to spend time alone. Mothers worry if their children don't have lots of friends. A "loner" carries the stigma of maladjustment. We're supposed to be always socializing, or at least part of a couple. Taking pleasure in being with yourself is considered anti-social, especially if yours is a deliberate preference. A friend phoned me yesterday and asked me to have lunch with her. When I said that I felt like being alone for most of the day, she replied, "What's the matter? What's wrong?" Being alone is acceptable if you're miserable (and thus spare others from your misery), but being alone is usually not equated with pleasure or choice.

Privacy, however, is not only a pleasure but a necessity. The lack of privacy is a major defect in almost all rehabilitation centers and nursing homes. Older people withdraw into isolation in order to protect what little privacy they have. In one nursing home they gave people private cubicles plus some adjoining social space, instead of the previous three-bed room arrangement. This provided both personal and private space. Research showed that socializing then increased significantly (Lawton, 1970).

All of us need time alone to integrate experiences into meaningful patterns and for self-exploration. Especially when we are "on the go," it's difficult to process the myriad information, events, and reactions that bombard our life. Privacy allows us to shape, retaste, assimilate, and integrate.

Being alone (not *being lonely*) is being with yourself. Once considered a developmental task of adolescence, defining the "self" can also be a task of aging. Retired people can have a self that they can't find. *Loneliness* is a complaint of older people who lack a sense of self and identity. Retirement and loss of socially structured roles, such as "worker" or "mother" or "housewife" can cause a person great discomfort, especially if no personal "inner core" has been developed. The problem for many older people today is that they never established a personal identity independent from their social roles. The unresolved developmental tasks of previous stages of life come back to plague the older person.

The more options an older person has—from both within the self and from society—the more likely it is that life will be satisfying and growing. For many people "life without an object to pursue is a languid and tiresome thing" (Sir Francis Bacon), and work provides the "object." Even laboratory rats get bored in an unchallenging environment.

The myth of Sisyphus symbolizes an important and valid lifestyle for some people:

> The gods had condemned Sisyphus to ceaselessly rolling a rock to the top of a mountain, whence the stone would fall back of its own weight. They had thought with some reason that there is no more dreadful punishment than futile and hopeless labor . . . (but) there is no fate that cannot be surmounted by scorn . . . . One does not discover the absurd without being tempted to write a manual of happiness . . . . Happiness and the absurd are two sons of the same earth . . . . One always finds one's burden again. But Sisyphus teaches the higher fidelity that negates the gods and raises rocks. He concludes that "all is well" . . . . The struggle itself toward the heights is enough to fill a man's heart.   *[Camus, 1955, pp. 90-91]*

For some people, the "struggle toward the heights" gives meaning to life. As Benjamin Franklin said, "There is nothing wrong with retirement as long as one doesn't allow it to interfere with one's work." For some people it does interfere. They need their jobs. Retirement can be a process of deculturation, in which the habits of a lifetime are reversed. Some cannot reset their goals. Hobbies, crafts, clubs, and inner-directed leisure are not enough.

MULTIPLE CAREERS AND LIFELONG EDUCATION

The concept of education continuing throughout life is relatively new in American education (Peterson, 1975). Traditionally, education has been geared to socialize youth and prepare them for adulthood. However, lifelong learning is becoming increasingly common and is finally being encouraged by colleges.

People are going to seek in the future not only more education but also multiple careers during a lifetime. As we mature, our interests can change. People increasingly refuse to live like machines that must do the same job year after year. Industry's expectations are changing, and already multiple careers are becoming an accepted reality. Literally millions of

Americans change occupations every year, and around half of these people are over the age of thirty-five.

The developmental task of the older person having to adjust to retirement may become extinct in the near future. Tomorrow's aged population will probably be substantially better educated, more socially conscious, and more politically active than today's. The young people who were involved in civil rights and student protest activities will more likely be a new type of "senior activist."

GRIEF AND MOURNING

> Happiness is beneficial for the body, but it is grief that ennobles the mind. *[Proust]*

Whether retirement occurs or not, there will be losses; your friends and peers die, your physical appearance and health change, roles and status are altered, and so on. And often the older person experiences a sense of loss and grief with each of these changes.

Grief is the work of getting through the pain of loss. You often learn a great deal from pain and the agony of loss. To move through grief you must express the tears, angers, disappointments, guilt, or despair. The biggest obstacle to mourning is that many people try to avoid the intense pain involved. Grief can be one of the most lonely, intense, and intimate events in a person's life. Almost without exception, when older people are asked for the saddest memory in their lives, they answer in terms of grief due to the death of a beloved (Roberts *et al.,* 1970). Interestingly, the death of one's mother is the most frequently cited loss, even more so than the loss of a spouse.

One of the worst aspects of grieving is when people do not connect their pain and misery with the loss, and they feel they are "going insane." They do not realize what they are experiencing is normal. People who have had a major loss should be told that they are in the process of grief and what the common symptoms are.

The first stage of grief for the death of a loved person is usually shock. A feeling of disbelief, of denial, and of numbness often lasts for several days. The person may have few emotions or tears. If tranquilizers are used, then this state of numbness can be prolonged, and the work of grief will be delayed. While nighttime sedation is often a good idea, so a person can rest, tranquilizers are seldom advisable.

Throughout the grief process, and especially during the early stage of numbness, the common body reactions are shortness of breath, a feeling of suffocation, weak knees, muscle weakness, and an emptiness in the pit of the stomach. Frequent, deep sighing is also a pronounced tendency. Insomnia and loss of appetite are common; a typical reaction to food is that it "tastes like sand."

The second stage of grieving often continues for twelve weeks, but can last up to a year. Once a person begins to come out of the shock and denial stage, and to express his or her feelings, any of the following symptoms are normal:

- The deceased is talked about in the present tense, as if still part of the living. Hallucinations and delusions of contact with the deceased may even occur.

- There may be a "cocoon response." A person may feel reluctant to travel away from home, display abnormally intense fear of being hurt, or worry about other family members being injured. The world is felt to be a dangerous place and life to be fragile. The feeling is that of wanting to crawl into bed (or some other safe place) and pull the sheets up over the head.

- The person who is grieving may have memory lapses or amnesia about what is happening around him/her. This often causes a person to feel as if he or she is going crazy.

- The bereaved feels there is nothing worthwhile to live for and experiences changes in sleeping, eating, sexual patterns, and elimination processes. Frequently, the person has trouble sleeping at night and will very likely wake up during the night. The bereaved does not recognize that these symptoms are due to depression.

- The bereaved person is preoccupied with the deceased. Sometimes, the preoccupation is acted out through some kind of "linking object" or token. For instance, one young man carried his father's raincoat around with him for several months after the father's death.
- Sometimes other people seem very small, shadowy, or unreal. Voices seem to come from a long way away.
- The bereaved may feel a disconcerting loss of warmth or concern toward other people. She or he may feel anger (why did this happen?), guilt (if only I had insisted on his/her seeing a doctor sooner), jealousy (why is her husband alive and not mine?), and irritability. The bereaved person can feel that he or she is evil or going insane because of this abnormal negativity toward others.

Any or all of these reactions during grieving are normal. The bereaved must know the typical symptoms and accept them, whatever their unique configuration may be.

The final stage of grief, usually within a year after the death, is its resolution. There is decreasing sadness, a resumption of ordinary life, and the ability to recall the past with pleasure as well as pain. Time and the ventilation of feelings are essential for getting to this stage of readjustment. The loss is still there, the scar remains. There will still be times of sadness, the cycles of grief, and the emotional outbursts. The future anniversaries of the death will probably be vulnerable times for the resurgence of emotions and memories. However, with time, the person moves toward adjustment and new relationships (adapted from White & Gathman, 1973).

Facilitating Grief and Mourning

Unfortunately, most bereaved people are still in a state of shock when social support is at its greatest, during the first few days or sometimes weeks after a death. Just about the time they are beginning to get in touch with their feelings of grief, friends and family are usually urging them to "get back to living." For this reason, most recovery from grief is done alone in our society.

Pain, like any sensation, is to be experienced. We can help ourselves, or others, to live through the process of grief by encouraging emotional release. Some people need to be helped; otherwise grieving can go on for years and become pathological. The following are a few suggestions for helping a person to grieve:

1. When a death occurs, unresolved and unsaid things often torment the bereaved. Writing a letter to the person who died, expressing what is being felt, may help. Obviously the letter will never be mailed or read by the deceased; it is simply a way of working through the "unfinished business." Putting your thoughts and feelings into a tangible form can be a tremendous release. It loosens the pain by giving it a form of expression.

2. A visit by the bereaved to the grave is often therapeutic. It increases the reality of the loss and consequently the intensity of mourning. In Jewish tradition a tombstone cannot be placed on a grave until eight weeks after a death, and then only in a ritual in which all of the bereaved participate. This event is often a highly emotional time, even more so than the funeral.

3. We need to have "grieving rooms" in hospitals that are soundproof and private. We need to socially sanction and encourage people to get in touch with their grief and to express it. Hospital and health professionals need to be trained so that they can help people, instead of encouraging repression.

4. Crisis intervention services can be extremely helpful. Communities need to develop more of these services, such as widow-to-widow groups, where one can share feelings and experiences with others who are sympathetic and going through the same experience.

ANTICIPATORY GRIEF

Anticipatory grief is a period of "rehearsal" for an impending loss. Prior to research, those who lost loved ones because of a death from chronic illness were supposedly better prepared to adjust than people faced with a sudden loss. We think of a sudden death as more tragic because the bereaved isn't given time to prepare, to say farewells, and to begin working through emotions. However, a recent study of grief and mourning demonstrates that the aged who were bereaved by a lengthy chronic fatal illness make a worse adjustment than those bereaved after a shorter chronic illness:

> Of those subjects whose relatives died of a fatal illness lasting longer than one year, sixty-eight percent had intense grief reactions, as compared to only thirty percent of those reporting either illness of less than one year's duration or death not preceded by illness.
> *[I. Gerber et al., 1975, p. 226]*

Anticipatory grief and preparation for a loss has limited adjustment value, particularly if this phase is not handled well —as is usually the case. Too much anticipation and "worry-work" seems to wear a person out, rather than help adjustment. It can be helpful if an older person who goes through a long anticipatory grief period can receive help in expressing feelings.

"LETTING GO" OF GRIEF

Accepting a loss and "letting go" of it is not a new experience that suddenly occurs late in life. We experience many farewells throughout life, such as discarded self-images, broken dreams, friends who move away, and parents who die. We let go of illusions. We are not as brilliant, talented, famous, all-loving, or sensitive as we had dreamed. We lose people and possessions throughout life, not just in old age. The major difference with aging is that when we are young the vacuum caused by a loss is usually filled immediately, often without any conscious effort. Opportunities for new people, new roles, and new experiences are seemingly unlimited.

With aging, limitations set in. For example, research indicates that less than 5 percent of women widowed after age 55 ever remarry (Cleveland & Gianturco, 1976). Often, turning inward is the only source of pleasure available for the older person. With age, therefore, ever more conscious efforts must be made to replace losses, often with something entirely different or new.

Perhaps Tillich's advice about adjusting to losses and letting go of the past is the most succinct and appropriate: "Stay open." No simple solutions exist for losses, other than to express the grief as the first step to recovery. Frequently, people wish to dispense with "difficult" or painful feelings like grief and anger; but to numb any strong feeling is to numb all feelings, including the pleasurable ones.

DEATH AND DYING/LIFE AND LIVING

> It is imperative that the older person should have a positive attitude toward death. The young can forget death with impunity. The old cannot.   *[Irene Claremont de Castillejo]*

Death is a total loss—the loss of the self. Adapting positively to the reality of your own death is one of the major tasks of aging. For younger people, foreseeable death is always a possibility. For the aged person, it becomes an increasing certainty.

Most older people rarely have an opportunity to discuss their feelings about death and dying with anyone. It is still a taboo subject, despite the large number of books written recently. A student asked the director of a Nevada nursing home, "When you ask older people about dying, how do they feel about death?" The director answered: "Don't ever ask, because they [the elderly patients] tend to get very, very upset."

In one of Nevada's largest hospitals attitudes are changing on the subject of death and dying. Cancer patients are encouraged to attend group sessions and to discuss their feelings about the subject; some of the hospital's professional staff have voluntarily attended workshops on death and dying. Nonetheless, this same hospital still uses falsebottom gurneys (the wheeled tables used to move patients) to disguise the death of a patient.

Customs for managing the death of a patient vary from one institution to another. But almost always death is treated as "dirty" and shameful. The nursing staff of one hospital are advised to go home "and wash up and change clothes" after touching the deceased. At one home for the aged in Nevada, with almost one hundred residents, the administration and staff pretend that they are having a fire drill when a patient dies; they *lock* patients into their rooms and clear the hallways, so that the deceased can be removed "without upsetting the patients"!

Just as with grief and mourning, most older people's fears about death and dying are worked out either alone or through denial. For most people, at any age, death is uncomfortable to think about. Imagining our "not being" is almost impossible. Fear of death is a paramount and pervasive reaction. Many older people acknowledge neither death nor their fear of it. If pressed, they say that they only hope to die in their sleep, which is tantamount to not having to even acknowledge death or endure a consciousness of it.

Yet often death is not feared so much as the dying process. Two questions the dying patient commonly asks (if given the opportunity) are: "Will there be pain?" and "Will I have to be alone?"

There are two types of grief: that which is for others and that which is directed toward yourself. Grieving for yourself and your own death is the prototype of anticipatory grief. Working through your feelings about death is similar to the process of grieving for others. It is painful but ". . . we can't live fully until we have faced our finiteness, our inevitable death. . . . Life is richest when we realize we are all snowflakes.

Each of us is absolutely beautiful and unique. And we are here for a very short time [Keen, 1975, p. 44]. Acceptance of your future "not being" can strengthen your art of "being now." Freud said, "If you want to enjoy life, prepare for death [Balint, 1956, p. 83]."

One technique for generating a greater sense of death's reality is to make out an "emotional will." This kind of will addresses itself not to financial matters in legalistic jargon, but to private and intimate subjects in personal and loving language. For example, a woman of 62 wrote the following emotional will:

> I'd like to leave my poems, which I have always been too embarrassed to show anyone, to my daughter. I would like my grandson to have my coin collection, with the hope that he will enjoy it as much as I have. It was given to me by my great-grandmother and has always been my special treasure. It was her special gift to me when I was a young girl and all that I have of her, an extraordinary woman. Next, I would like to leave my red travel case to J. P. R., my close friend, in hopes that she may find it useful when she explores those places that I will never be able. I would also like her to have my Japanese earrings, in memory of our wonderful friendship and reckless youth spent together. I would like my husband to have my antique vase, that I've always loved most, with the hope that he will find beauty and grow anew.

Most older people, because of the "conspiracy of silence" surrounding them about death and dying, are denied the opportunity or encouragement to reach a resolution with others about their death. Writing an "emotional will" and sharing it is one way of bridging the silence.

The person who acknowledges death can begin to experience a sense of immediacy, of living each moment:

> This can be called a sense of "presentness." The elemental things of life—children, plants, nature, human touching—assume greater significance as people sort out the more important from the less important. Old age . . . can be a time of emotional and sensory awareness and enjoyment.   *[Butler & Lewis, 1973, p. 25]*

Abraham Maslow, psychologist and author, after recovering from a heart attack spoke clearly to the issue of death and dying, of life and living, and how they are all intertwined. After his illness, "life was a bonus and everything—flowers, friendships, the very act of living—became more beautiful." He had a "much-intensified sense of miracles [Kaluger & Kaluger, 1974, p. 306]." Just before his death he was recorded to have said, "If you're reconciled with death . . . then every single moment of every single day is transformed because the pervasive undercurrent—the fear of death—is removed [p. 306]."

Some older people. realizing they have a finite number of years ahead, become "life seekers." Time takes on a different meaning. Interestingly enough, the more spontaneously an older person lives, the more he or she savors and perceives time as moving more slowly. Older people perceive themselves as having less time available in the future; thus they tend to seek gratification now, rather than delay it (Lynch, 1971). This new insight can be one of the advantages of growing older!

Every moment of life, as Maslow indicated, can be seen as a gift. Learning to accept death is not only part of life but an enrichment of living. If our lives went on forever, if there were no death, then we might well postpone our gratifications and "sense of presentness" forever. Our knowledge of death-is one of our most powerful tools for full, pleasurable living. Our bodies live only in the present. That openness to the present is precisely what the older person must strive for.

STAGES IN DYING/DYING IN STAGES

As people live through the process of dying, they develop many moods and feelings, ranging from eager and curious to panicked and outraged. Several efforts have been made to define stages that most people go through during this process, the most noteworthy being the well-known five stages described with great insight by Elisabeth Kubler-Ross (1969). However, the general consensus of persons who spend most of their time working with the dying is that very few people die in the stages as outlined (Kastenbaum, 1977). Each person dies a unique death in an individual fashion. Your death is as unique a part of you as any other facet of your life.

Nonetheless, several moods often set in during the dying process, especially when it is an observable downhill trajectory (as with cancer), rather than an erratic trajectory (as a major coronary, a stroke, an automobile accident, or a suicide). These moods include Ross' five stages (denial and isolation, anger and resentment, bargaining and postponing, depression and sense of loss, acceptance and quiet expectation). Other moods include fear, curiosity, frustration, extreme dependency, withdrawal, and gentle sadness.

People die, it is often said, as they lived. But this saying may be more of a platitude than a careful observation. Indeed, some people carry ongoing characteristics throughout their lives and into their deaths, but others are more open to change. Sometimes death overcomes a previously emotionally strong and capable person, changing that individual's personality completely; at other times, immense personal growth occurs in the face of death.

Do the old die differently than the non-old? The answer is a cautious "yes." According to what older people have told research investigators, they are less afraid of death and dying, but they think about it more often (Kalish & Reynolds, 1976).

Although some health professionals claim that such statements merely underline how much the elderly deny their own death, it is more likely that the research findings are accurate. Three basic reasons have been given: First, the elderly have limited futurity—society and their own health often make life less desirable; second, old people have lived as long as they had expected to, that is, they have received what they felt entitled to; third, older people have had so many experiences with the deaths of others that they have learned to live with dying. They expect to die and they accept death, having worked through its terror and anguish many times before as they suffered the grief of loss (Kalish, 1976).

Regardless of specific feelings and attitudes, dying people of any age can be helped by those who love them. The needs of a dying person, just like the needs of any other person, include receiving basic physiological necessities, feeling safe and secure (not likely to be abandoned), feeling loved and esteemed (not deserted), and feeling that growth is possible even during the dying process. The search for growth can come through the search for meaning, and facing death challenges the meaning of meaning itself.

SENSATION, SEX, AND PLEASURE

> Our obsession with achievement pervades our sexual lives. We strive to perfect the "product" orgasm, and ignore the pleasures of leisurely love . . . work and sex are natural enemies, and the more personal commitment the work generates, the more inroads it makes into erotic life . . . eroticism tends to become perfunctory—a release rather than a pasttime. . . . Discussions of sexuality in America have always centered on the orgasm rather than on pleasure in general . . . . The antithetical attitude would be to view orgasm as a delightful interruption in an otherwise continuous process of generating pleasurable sensations . . . people we view as particularly alive are those capable of sustaining a lot of pleasurable stimulation without discharging it or blunting their senses.
>
> *[Slater, 1973, p. 17–18]*

The sensory and sexual losses that occur with aging can be the most personally devitalizing and annihilating of all. It is a partial death of the self, in which people, grieving for the loss of a significant aspect of themselves, go through many of the symptoms of mourning, especially depression. A healthy but impotent 72-year-old widower writes:

> I have not slept with any woman or man (I add the latter with almost humor, for I cannot conceive of homosexuality in any form)

for over two years. During these two years I have noted deterioration physically, emotionally, and mentally. I have little desire to live
as I live . . . . I'll probably soon make an effort to find the border-
line of death . . . life has no pleasure for me . . . being alone hurts.
Without being able to make love, my life is barren. I am hungry for
touch and hate my body that is useless for what my mind still
hungers.   *[Anonymous]*

The myth that older people have no sexual desires and are
impotent is dangerous: It can become a self-fulfilling prophecy
in which sexual needs become a problem rather than a joy. Fortunately, several excellent books, written recently, debunk
these myths about aging and sexuality (Butler & Lewis, 1976;
Peterson & Payne, 1975).

The supposed loss of interest in sex and impotency are
often socially, rather than biologically, induced. Recent studies
show that people can usually remain sexually active well into
their eighties (Masters & Johnson, 1966). And when sexual
problems do occur, research indicates that the aged person can
be helped with counseling. Masters and Johnson (1970) report that they are able to restore potency in 65 percent of their
elderly male patients.

Biofeedback (see Chapter 5) is also being used to solve
problems of impotency in the aged; mastering some of the so-
called involuntary functions, such as brain waves and blood
pressure, can also apply to erections (Popov, 1975).

Mary Sviland has been engaged in running a sex therapy
program especially for people over the age of 60. The flood of
applicants for her program indicates that the aged, contrary
to stereotypes, are very much interested in their sexuality.
Using modern sex therapy techniques, Sviland has found
that treatment for sexual dysfunctions with older persons can
prove to be "remarkably successful within weeks." However,
she has also found that aging does change and slow down
sexuality. Many older couples must be helped to free themselves from what she calls the "touch-down mentality" of
sex American style. They should learn to accept the idea that

love play and pleasure can be enjoyed in themselves and do not always have to end in orgasm (Sviland, 1975).

With aging, the concept of sex has to be extended from the genitals to include sensuality. *Sensuality* means an involvement of the entire body, with tactile voluptuousness and luxurious stimulation of the senses as a way of love-making. The lack of pleasure orientation in our society contributes greatly to sexual dysfunctions: We tend to focus on the brief pleasure or orgasm, instead of on the process. Eroticism exists mostly with leisurely, nongoal-directed sensuous activity enjoyed for itself.

Sensory Losses

Sensory acuity often declines with growing older, possibly due to deficits in the peripheral sensory systems. Botwinick (1973) makes it clear: "Probably in no other area of psychological investigation are the findings so clearcut and consistent: old people simply don't see, hear, or otherwise perceive as acutely as do younger people [p. 120]."

Adjustment to sensory loss is a vital adjustment task of successful aging. Sensuality and "touch hunger" become even more important because of these losses. A brief review of sensory losses that may occur with aging might be helpful.

With age, visual acuity (the ability to see clearly at a distance) can decline, along with a loss in ability to focus on near objects (Botwinick, 1973). Seeing in the dark also becomes more difficult—a situation that can be dangerous for the older person who drives or walks at night (Kimmel, 1974). By age 70, most people have some significant visual problem.

Hearing also changes for many people. Most commonly, the ability to hear high pitch tones declines. The loss of hearing, however, may not be a normal part of aging. In less industrialized and quieter societies, hearing is almost as keen in old age as it is in youth (MacFarland, 1968). Hearing loss among our aged, thought to be attributable in part to our noise pollution, is becoming prevalent. A recent National Health Survey indicates that 30 percent of our older people suffer a significant hearing loss (Butler & Lewis, 1973, p. 97).

A significant relationship may also exist between the degree of hearing loss and personality functioning. Depression and paranoia are the most common emotional consequences of hearing loss because of fears produced by the sense of isolation from others (Butler & Lewis, p. 97). In addition, people may experience irritability, suppression of feelings, withdrawal, and poor organization of daily behavior. Even limited losses can bring significant personality and social problems. Background noises, such as traffic, birds singing, the wind, and so on, seem to be necessary for maintaining mental health. Without these subliminal sounds, an older person "will feel a sense of loss, a feeling that the world is dead [Winter, 1973, p. 49]." So behavior that seems sensile or psychotic may be triggered by hearing loss. Increasing other sensory stimulation can help to compensate.

Sensitivity to taste and smell is generally thought to decrease with aging. About two-thirds of the taste buds in the mouth die by the age of 70; a large proportion of sensory receptors in the nose have also died by this age (Woodruff, 1975, p. 193). A recent study (Schiffman, 1975) concluded that older people were significantly poorer at taste identifications. However, an older person can learn to compensate, as evidenced by the fact that most gourmets, brewmeisters, and tasters are older people. The evidence regarding taste and smell losses is not unequivocal (Botwinick, 1973, p. 126). They seem to be culturally attuned senses that can be stimulated to maintain a high level of functioning.

The sense of touch (touch sensitivity) appears to decline around the age of 50 (Botwinick, 1973, p. 127). However, "data are noticeably absent in the area of tactile sensitivity" with aging (Botwinick, p. 127).

In general, most people receive less sensory input as they age. Losses in sight and hearing can especially cause an older person to hesitate in relating to the world, due to a loss of confidence in bearings. If deprived of sensory sharpness in any way, a person would logically then need increased stimulation of all kinds to compensate. More "in-touchness" becomes a vitally necessary way of relating to the world.

Seven

THE PLEASURES
OF AGING

Life is a banquet and most people starve to death.

[Author unknown]

Old age doesn't have to be a tragedy, but our society can
make it so. Old people are often treated as useless discards,
forced to retire and often to live in poverty. The older, retired
persons living in America are the largest poor minority in this
country, with the greatest deprivation of basic needs. United
States government statistics for 1975, published in 1977, show
that 15 percent of older persons live in poverty. (Poverty was
defined as an income of under $2,600 a year for a single, older,
person, and $3,250 for a married couple with the head of
household over 65.)

As a society, our outlook still is distorted by the puritanical bias that life without productivity is meaningless. By pressuring the elderly into retirement without adequate income, we strip them of status and esteem. Very few nursing homes offer adequate psychological and social resources; in many communities, resources for the elderly are nonexistent. Publicly, older people are often imprisoned in a roleless role (Wood, 1971) and regarded as persons-about-to-die. The trend in industrial societies has been toward a change in the family structure that once provided the elderly with protection, housing, and respect. Because of these social factors and a lack of inner resources, many older people withdraw into a shell that can become an early coffin.

The only alternatives are to reject society's assumptions about the worth of being older and to develop the inner resources with which to create new values.

Never before in history could we better afford to develop a more humane philosophy of life. Productivity has always been a matter of survival. Today it's different. This is a pivotal time for change. As Julian Huxley has said: "The leisure problem is fundamental. Having to decide what we will do with our leisure is inevitably forcing us to re-examine the purpose of human existence, and to ask what fulfillment really means."

Older people living today are the first generation to deal with a reality of leisure and retirement. Free time, for pleasure and leisure, is a relatively new phenomenon. In 1870, the standard American work week was seventy hours; in 1900, it was fifty-five hours; today, it is thirty-eight hours. Our working hours have been reduced by an average of three hours per decade since 1900. This means that compared to our grandfathers, work is a smaller part of our lives, and it is expected to be even less in the future (Peterson, 1973, p. 20).

The major revolution in our time is a shift from a work-centered world to a leisure-dominated life (Peterson, p. 20). For the first time in human history, in industrialized countries, service industries are exceeding production industries. Services such as travel, food, education, social services, finance, medicine, and recreation account for over half of our gross national product. Also, for the first time in history most people will spend more years at leisure than at work. Industrial marketing, sales, and advertising acknowledge this trend and try to ring it up on the cash register by tying leisure to the consumption of material goods, such as buying the best and latest recreational equipment or the most luxurious mobile home. For 1976, *U.S. News and World Report* estimated that Americans would spend $130 billion on sporting activities. The *Reno Evening Gazette* (April 22, 1976) comments:

> This leisure and recreation business is really getting to be big stuff. One way to measure the growing interest in recreation and leisure is the existence of this page. Ten years ago, you'd be hard-pressed to find any one page in a daily newspaper devoted entirely to recreation. Another even more accurate gauge is the changing curriculum in our colleges and universities . . . it's unbelievable . . . [the universities believe that] we're experiencing a whole change of lifestyle. People are devoting more time to recreation . . . it may seem strange to "learn" how to jog or ride a bike . . . [but the university is] trying to orientate students to the fact that it's important to play for the pure pleasure of it.   *[p. 15]*

THE TASK OF PLEASURING

> Only the old are capable of savouring pleasure soberly, thoroughly and with complete absorption.   *[Balint, 1956]*

Pleasure is the key to health and the essence of living fully. Pleasure is a celebration of the self and a style of relating to others. Some people have the ability to make life a series of exhilarations in which they have a love affair with living. For such people, the inevitable losses that occur with aging are genuine, deep sorrows rather than dramatized tragedies frozen into a role. People who have not developed resources for pleasuring tend to experience life—and especially the stages of aging—as a burden.

In our society, pleasure is usually spoken of with a note of apology or defensiveness. Pleasure, sensuousness, joy, happiness, delight, ease, and enjoyment are haunting emotions, because so much guilt is associated with feeling good. We usually allow ourselves pleasure only if we "deserve" it by working for it. Why do we have to justify it by work? Why do we feel that too much self-pleasuring is evil?

To act conspicuously cheerful or to tell someone that you're feeling joyful is sometimes to invite silence and a skeptical look, as if you're being "shallow." The wordless accusation is that you must be holding back the truth. The social expectation is that the sorrows of life—that is, our surgical operations and emotional scars—are the primary, or "real," experiences.

We need to stop apologizing for feeling good. When something is pleasurable for adults, we classify it as recreation. Recreation is from the Latin word *recreare,* which means to restore or to refresh. The American's inference is that pleasure isn't legitimate in its own right but must be a re-creation of energy for getting back to the serious business of life: work. For people oriented toward a life of work, pleasure may represent a dangerous seduction away from productivity. It can evoke ambivalence within a person, a conflict between the free-child part of you and the stern parent-adult.

It also has its risks. We often hold ourselves back from allowing pleasurable feelings because we're afraid of the pain of losing them or of disappointment. It's "safer" to stay away from expecting or wanting pleasure.

Pleasure is one of the most neglected subjects in psychology. *Psychological Abstracts,* a professional journal that indexes all articles written every year in the field of psychology, classifies over twelve thousand articles each year. In 1975, from all the various professional psychology journals, only twenty articles were indexed under the categories of Pleasure, Joy, Happiness, and Fun. The same year, approximately five hundred articles were written on the subject of depression! Our focus remains on the pathological rather than the positive aspects of psychology.

". . . [T] he theory of the happy life has remained at about the level where the Greek philosophers left it [Wilson, 1967, p. 302]." Few modern efforts of theoretical or practical interest have been made in psychology regarding pleasure.

What is pleasure? *Webster's New Collegiate Dictionary* (1974) defines pleasure as "a source of delight or joy." *Webster's New World Dictionary* (1959) defines it as "one's wish, will, or choice; a thing that gives delight or satisfaction." Pleasure includes involvements covering the whole range of human life. It is composed of a feeling state and, more broadly, of experiences. Pleasure may find expression in athletics, social interaction, games, play, contemplation, curiosity, giving service to others, being with nature, art, sensuousness, intellectual pursuits, and work. Later in this chapter is a list of almost 150 activities usually considered pleasurable. However, like stress, pleasure is not inherent in any activity; it is, rather, inherent in the person. It is the person's positive response to experiences.

THE PROBLEM WITH HAPPINESS

Happiness is usually more specific; you are usually happy "about something." It is often a transcendental experience, a suspension of ordinary reality. Happiness therefore has only a limited meaning: It is a feeling state described by a noun or an adjective, but not by a verb. By contrast, the word "pleasure" can become a verb. "Pleasuring" is the giving, seeking, or taking of pleasure.

Happiness also implies a certain passivity; it usually simply happens to us. Pleasuring, on the other hand, is "one's wish, will or choice." Our pleasures are of our own choosing and, therefore, of our own responsibility.

Pleasure, not limited to an intense "flow" or peak experience, is more difficult to accept. A pleasurable activity tends to be something with which you choose to become involved, while happiness is often something that overcomes us and for which we aren't therefore necessarily responsible.

> It is not necessary to have fun or to be happy to experience plea-
> sure. One can have pleasure in the ordinary circumstances of life,
> for pleasure is a mode of being . . . a person is in a state of pleasure
> . . . in harmony with his surroundings.   *[Lowen, 1970]*

Pleasure can be a prevailing mood of enjoying your life, your activities, the exercise of your ability, your striving for growth, your relations with others, and your involvement with society in general. Putting the focus of living on the subjective experience of pleasuring doesn't imply a restriction of choices.

UTILITARIAN AND PURE PLEASURES

Most of us were brought up with a utilitarian attitude toward pleasure, in which pleasure, as a temporary exemption from work, must first be deserved and earned. In this context, danc-ing is fine for keeping limber, playing bridge sharpens the mind, hiking keeps you physically fit, golf provides social contacts, and so on. Even children's play is justified in terms of "growing up and rehearsing adult roles" rather than as the spontaneous freedom it actually is. Everything that is fun, in other words, must also serve some useful purpose.

A contrasting approach to pleasure is to regard it simply as a time of joy. This approach is a rejection of the work ethic assumption that every investment of energy must produce a *useful* result. Viewed from a nonutilitarian perspective, pleasure is a rightful part of life. Whether it is good for your health or "therapeutic," whether it increases competence, or whether it gives energy becomes incidental. Pleasure is a worthy end in itself. Undeserved and unearned pleasure is commonly referred to as "pure pleasure." Some of us allow it so rarely in our lives that it becomes an experience of exhilaration when it does happen, a total engrossment in which a flowing of your self and time merge into one.

We make a distinction here between utilitarian and pure pleasure because of its implications for our living and aging. The difficulty with a utilitarian justification of pleasure is that *it limits how much and under what conditions* pleasure is allowable in our lives. As we age, we are fully capable and deserving of both kinds of pleasure.

> We must break away from the obsession with virtue that makes us sick and forbids us the joys of life.[1]

Pleasure and work are not necessarily contradictory. Work can be a pleasure. For most people, however, even if the work itself is pleasurable, the pressure associated with it makes it otherwise. Essentially pleasurable activity may become unpleasurable when it is hurried or pressured. Too often the creative, pleasant aspects of work are lost because of time-pressures and deadlines, the demand of having to produce. The contradictions between work and pleasure, when they exist, are contrasted in Table 7–1.

TABLE 7–1

Work versus Pleasure Activities

Work Activities	Pleasurable Activities
• goal-directed/controlled planning for the future	• spontaneous; focused on the present
• restraint, a deliberating state	• feeling of freedom, an experiential state
• provides material goods, responsive to external demands	• no external demands
• duty, obligation, responsibility	• voluntary

[1] Carl Jung, *Letters, Vol. I,* G. Adler, ed. (Princeton, N.J.: Princeton University Press, 1973), p. 17.

TABLE 7-1 (*cont.*)

Work Activities	Pleasure Activities
• deferred gratification	• a state of experiencing gratification and living in the moment
• interaction is intellectual or physical; low priority on emotional interaction	• interaction may be physical, emotional, or intellectual—and a combination of all
• conforming to rules	• creative, innovative
• routine	• freshness, discovery, newness
• utilitarian, a means to an end	• nonutilitarian, an end in itself
• defined as a virtue by society	• often regarded as sinful
• the basis of our economic system	• outside of and incidental to materialism
• ego-oriented	• body- and/or mind-oriented

Pleasure is an emotion or state that must be developed within ourselves, for which we must then find a context or content. For some fortunate people, their pleasure may merge with their work.

THE SOCIAL FEAR OF PLEASURE

To be a human being it is essential that an individual have the intelligence to control and select his pleasures.

[Joseph Fletcher, 1975, p. 15]

Part of the social stigma of pleasure is a fear of its potential danger to traditional social values. It not only defies the work ethic but also touches upon our attitudes toward spontaneity and the implied loss of control. In the extreme, a loss of control can manifest itself in destructive anti-social action, such as sadism or killing. The sanction and institutionalization of sadism and killing through warfare is not generally acknowledged, much less associated with pleasure. Culturally, we are distrustful and suspicious about what can happen if we fail to "control ourselves."

The concept of pleasure, as used here, means that we sometimes "lose control" of ourselves. However, though we may lose a sense of consciousness and deliberation, we picture pleasure as occurring in ways that will not cause harm. There is a subtle art in surrendering to the moment without abdicating responsibility and realistic control. Pleasure or displeasure of some sort enters into every moral situation. As ethical human beings, we have to consider what makes certain enjoyments and pleasures worthier than others. We cannot evade this problem. Part of validating positive and creative pleasure is the search for ethical behavior and personal integrity in relation to others.

In the final analysis, pleasure needs to be a way of celebrating reality based on appropriate choices, rather than a way of escaping reality and the need for choices. For example, the "pleasure" of being drunk is an escape from consciousness; its pleasure lies in the removal of the self from the world as it exists. So do many other self-abusive excesses. Escaping into mindlessness can scarcely be considered pleasurable when the person is not sufficiently conscious and aware of what is going on to enjoy the experience.

Pleasure does not have to be destructive to earn a negative image. Today, a few elderly people who have the courage to be pleasure seekers are referred to by certain health professionals as "neurotics" who have "undesirable regression," who are "impulsive," and who are "dominated by the pleasure principle." Their pleasure-orientation, in itself, is considered pathological. Why not consider these geriatric delinquents—who have the fortitude to maintain a zest for living, who refuse to be caged in by others' opinions—as our heroes and heroines? They meet with disapproval because we are "victims of a moral epidemic [that has] . . . yielded to the success compulsion which, though depriving us of daily happiness, is a possession we are incapable of exorcising [Szasz, 1957, p. 186]."

The stigma is carried over, of course, into old age by the elderly themselves. Many older people restrain their impulsiveness and pleasure-orientation for fear of being considered "social deviates." Research has shown that the elderly, as a group, are the most judgmental and unaccepting of their peers' unconventional behavior. Many older persons are so insecure about their status and self-esteem that they become ultra-obedient to social mores, hoping thereby to earn acceptance. For example, older people, more than any other age group, disapprove of the following behaviors: a retired couple who wear shorts when they go shopping, a recently widowed woman of 65 who buys a red convertible automobile, a retired couple who frequently attend nightclubs with a floor show (Wood, 1971). When it comes to allowing ourselves to enjoy life, we are all our own worst enemies.

PURE PLEASURE AND HEDONISM

> [We are] handicapped by the fact that the culture we live in is not oriented toward creative activity and pleasure . . . it is not geared to the values and rhythms of the living body but to those of machines and material productivity.   *[Lowen, 1975, p. 50]*

It is easy to become disgusted and feel imprisoned by our society's traditional work orientation, and swing the opposite way. Over-praising old age and over-reacting to society's work ethics are also understandable tendencies. But they do not help us to arrive at a realistic plan for actual living.

Today we are experiencing an intermingling of emerging norms, typifed by the descendents of those we once called hippies, with the old, traditional work ethic. We do not wish to denigrate old values, such as work, but we do wish to elevate the value placed on other uses of time.

Time is life. To "kill time" is murder. Most of us unfortunately have been taught to run away from time rather than to live in the present. We forget our pasts, preserving a disconnected series of memories. Our present moments are often bartered for the future. We become mesmerized by our anticipations. The present is rarely allowed to exist. With pleasuring activities, however, we become alive in the "now." Every pleasure is a new one, and no two are identical.

The single most important thing we can learn for successful aging is to give pleasure to ourselves and others.

Pleasuring means accepting some of the value of hedonism, an ancient Greek philosophy that advocates pleasure as the sole or chief good in life. (*Heidonei* is an ancient Greek word meaning "pleasure.") In the Christian era, this philosophy became simplified to indicate only erotic experiences of "wine, women, and song." Carnal pleasure has always been considered the main temptation of the devil, an evil thing. *Webster's New World Thesaurus* (1971) gives many synonyms for "hedonist": "sensualist, libertine, profligate, man of pleasure, pleasure-lover, thrill-seeker, voluptuary, rake, debaucher, epicurean, glutton, lecher." The definition reflects a sense of moral indignation, to say the least.

Before recoiling at the thought of becoming a hedonist, we should understand what the original philosophy meant for the Greeks.

The Epicureans, for example, stressed intellectual and moral satisfactions as the path to pleasure. Epicureanism, the philosophy of Epicurus, preached the quiet pleasures, so that one could seek peace of soul. It did not advocate an uncritical pursuit of pleasure. The ideal was to select enjoyments wisely, so as to achieve contentment. "Eat, drink, and be merry" was not originally a doctrine of random, passionate indulgence. To Epicurus it meant eat lightly, drink water, and enjoy philosophical conversation. This brand of hedonistic ethic held that intellectual pleasures were superior; it also advocated the renunciation of momentary pleasures in favor of long-range ones. This school contrasted with other types of hedonism devoted to sensual pleasure.

Plato, on the other hand, condemned physical pleasure as "base" compared to the "noble" pleasures of the mind. The body was rejected because of the "inferior soul" below the neck (Fletcher, 1975).

These extreme views had in common the agreement that a full life should contain as much pleasure as possible.

The concepts of hedonism and pleasure have been divided into unrealistic either-or divisions between mind and body, self and others, short-ranged and long-ranged categories. While to live for the pleasures of the moment is desirable, to have goals, to work for achievement, and to want success are also desirable. Both aims are fine and *do not have to be mutually exclusive.*

Part of the stimulation in our lives is provided by moving from one to the other, from work to pleasure. A life of short-ranged sensual hedonism would be too alien and shallow for most of us. We need some connection with the world, some unpleasurable compromises, some striving for goals. Some kind of coherence between ourselves and our relationship to the rest of humanity is essential. Likewise, it can be said that there must be pain for there to be pleasure, that life is a series of contrasts. Pleasure can be chiaroscuro—light and shade. The Sufis say that the secret of life is neither in the self nor in society, neither inside nor outside—but in moving from one to the other.

The problem in living with a dual philosophy is that society generally gives positive reinforcement only for delaying gratifications. This kind of reinforcement then becomes a pattern of living for tomorrow, and as a result today doesn't happen. We lose the capacity to experience the immediate and to exult in the present. We are taught to work for the good of society and others.

I asked a 68-year-old woman, "What gives you the most pleasure in your life right now?" She answered, "Giving to others." Yet her life is spent in front of a TV, bitterly waiting for others to ask her to give to them, and feeling like a failure because her children no longer want anything from her. A life of living for others, of too much dedication to work—a life without self-hedonism—will age into an empty receptacle. Our lives are the sum of the projects we choose. We are taught the virtue of giving to others and to society, but why not also give to ourselves?

Lowen (1970) makes this point most emphatically:

> Pleasure demands a serious attitude toward life, a commitment to one's existence . . . . Pleasure is the creative force in life . . . it is the only force strong enough to oppose the potential destructiveness of power . . . pleasure binds us to our bodies, to reality, to our friends, and to our work. *[p. 23]*

ONE MAN'S VIEWS

In developing this manuscript, I talked with many people about what it was like to be old, especially what kinds of pleasures came with old age. None of those I talked with impressed me as much as Abraham Feinberg, a man of seven distinct and distinguished careers in his 78 years: rabbi, radio romantic-tenor star, author, pop-album singer, anti-war activist, social-justice advocate, is currently writing his third book while vigorously espousing the cause of the elderly, his seventh career. Here are some excerpts from our discussions.

ABE: [T]he thing we should be liberated from most of all is our own self-subjugation. The elderly unconsciously accept the estimate the world has of them, and this becomes their estimate of themselves. We hear so much downgrading of the elderly image that we begin to believe it.

LIL: One of the main points I hope to convey is that "old is beautiful!" Abe, you come across as so energetic and zestful that you become beautiful.

ABE: Thank you, Lil. My zest for living is based on my religion, my philosophy, and my temperament. Despite all, I'm a Jew who will sing and dance and rejoice in life and love. Judaism is primarily a pragmatic, here-and-now religion that focuses on living: "One world at a time!"

There have been all kinds of disappointments and difficulties—and real, ancestral poverty—to overcome, and my own temperament to grapple with. But one of my beliefs says that we
should accept the gifts of life and enjoy them. We are in the house
of God and it is impolite not to take pleasure in what your host
has to offer you; it's discourtesy to the Creator to reject the
pleasures of life.

To know life is to love it. I know life. I know the dark and
discouraging and the melancholy side. I'm withdrawn sometimes.
I can be introspective and very remote. This has been part of my
nature. Especially after my wife died, I was in very bad shape.
Imprisoned in my dark side. But I snapped out of it when I realized it was a matter of life or death. I wanted to keep alive, not
fade out—to get re-involved—and my zest for living won out.

LIL: How has aging affected you?

ABE: I can maintain a full, intense lifestyle despite the fact that age is
creeping up on me, with some infirmities, aches, and pains. I've
started to develop arthritis. I'm not as agile as I used to be. But joy
for living is rooted deep. That tides me over, no matter what. I
enjoy what I'm doing. I love to sing and laugh and make speeches
and deal with ideas. I like listening to music. I relish being with a
good-looking woman.

LIL: Are you doing any kind of work for pay?

ABE: My career now is doing voluntary work and following my passionate interests. I prefer not being paid. I'm a free man. I could
get a job singing but I don't want it. I'd rather have less money.
There's a freedom in not being paid that elderly people with sufficient income are not taking advantage of. I don't have to be sub-
servient. And most important of all, I can speak my mind . . . .
Well, I've always done that!

LIL: What are some of the other freedoms that come with being old?

ABE: Unfortunately, most old people have too much freedom. They're
on their own, but with a sense of being useless. They don't know
how to use their leisure. The older you get, the more leisure you're
going to have. Leisure has to be happy, but how many people
know how?

LIL: I notice that sometimes when you talk about aging, you speak
about it almost as if you don't include yourself. Do you feel "old?"

ABE: No, most of the time I don't, at least not in any negative sense,
which is the way the word is too often used. As long as I have my
enthusiasm and zest for living, I feel ageless, a human being, not a
member of an age classification. They say that most people mellow

as they get older. That's just another way of saying they give in to spiritual and intellectual corrosion. The older I get, the more radical I become and the more outspoken about what's going on in our world.

PLEASURING, ACTIVITIES, AND AGING

Abraham Feinberg demonstrates that the ability to take pleasure obviously helps the older person cope successfully with life's changes. It is a vital adapting technique that is usually omitted from discussions about the "tasks of aging." In examining the life changes that occur with aging, we will find that the capacity for pleasure is one of the major growth needs of maturation. *Once we accept the importance of pleasuring, we are dealing not only with the plight of growing old but also with the opportunities.*

The whole dimension of "other senses," such as the stimulation of the pleasure sense, remains to be energetically developed and highly utilized for the full enjoyment of life. The ability to derive pleasure can help a person to adjust successfully to life's changes. The person who has a pleasant involvement with the present is not likely to look backwards and cling to the past. Successful aging implies the ability to replace losses with new satisfactions.

Which activities give pleasure? How do older people compare to younger people in the quantity and quality of pleasures utilized? How do healthy older people compare to depressed peers in these activities? What happens to our capacity for pleasure as we age?

I have developed a Pleasurable Activities Questionnaire[2] in which people of different ages were asked about activities that are pleasant experiences for them (see Figure 7–1). Many items

[2] I wish to acknowledge the prior work of Professors P. M. Lewinsohn and D. J. MacPhillamy in this area, reflected in their *Pleasant Events Schedule,* 1971.

Figure 7-1. Pleasurable Activities Questionnaire.

	Compared to 5 years ago, I enjoy this activity:			I wish that this activity would occur:			Check if not applicable
CREATIVE OR SELF-EXPRESSIVE ACTIVITIES	LESS	SAME	MORE	LESS	SAME	MORE	
1. Growing houseplants							
2. Redecorating my house or office							
3. Working in the yard or garden							
4. Working with my hands: sewing, knitting, needlework							
5. Playing, singing, or arranging music							
6. Photography							
7. Being in a play							
8. Doing creative art work such as painting, designing, sculpture, movie-making							
9. Craft work, such as making jewelry, pottery, leather, beads, weaving							
10. Collecting, such as stamps, coins, shells, rocks							
11. Finding a new hobby							
12. Doing creative writing; poetry stories, plays							
13. Writing letters, cards, diary, or journal							
14. Cooking, baking or canning							
15. Woodworking, carpentry, automechanics							
16. Fixing or repairing things							
17. Doing housework, making things clean							
18. Other:							
ACTIVITIES INVOLVING THE GIVING OF SERVICE TO OTHERS							
1. Donating something for a good cause							
2. Working in politics							
3. Joining a new organization							
4. Being active in community service projects— religious, charitable, or volunteer work							

153

	Compared to 5 years ago, I enjoy this activity:			I wish that this activity would occur:			Check if not applicable
. . . GIVING OF SERVICE TO OTHERS (cont.)	LESS	SAME	MORE	LESS	SAME	MORE	
5. Being an officer in an organization or club							
6. Being an active member in an organization or club							
7. Listening or advising on problems							
8. Other:							
WORK-OR JOB-RELATED ACTIVITIES							
1. Working at my trade or profession							
2. Doing something useful							
3. Being appreciated for my work							
4. Feeling important							
5. Getting status							
6. Having something to do							
7. Getting paid; being financially independent							
8. Playing "hookey" from work or school							
9. Other:							
ACTIVITIES OF SOCIAL INVOLVEMENT: Family, Friends, Community							
1. Talking or writing about old times— my personal past							
2. Talking about my health or my problems to someone who cares							
3. Eating out							
4. Having a picnic							
5. Being with my family							
6. Being with children							
7. Spending time with friends							
8. Remembering a departed friend or loved one; visiting the cemetery							
9. Long conversations on the telephone							

	Compared to 5 years ago, I enjoy this activity:			I wish that this activity would occur:			Check if not applicable
ACTIVITIES OF SOCIAL INVOLVEMENT: Family, Friends, Community (cont.)	LESS	SAME	MORE	LESS	SAME	MORE	
10. Finding a new friend or lover							
11. Dating, courting, or flirting							
12. Going to or giving parties							
13. Entertaining friends at home							
14. Going to church functions							
15. Going to a bar, tavern, nightclub, floorshow							
16. Hitchhiking, or picking up a hitchhiker							
17. Having a good conversation							
18. Being recognized as sexually attractive							
19. Sharing humor; having a good laugh							
20. Shocking people, swearing or flaunting different ideas for the fun of it							
21. Saying "no" to someone's request							
22. Directing or organizing people to do something							
23. Knowing that I am appreciated or needed—getting "strokes"							
24. Other:							
SPORTS OR ATHLETIC ACTIVITIES							
1. *Water Sports:* Swimming, surfing snorkeling, scuba diving, boating, sailing, canoeing, water skiing							
2. *Earth Sports:* Hiking, camping, rock climbing, fishing, kite flying							
3. *Animal Sports:* Bird watching, horseback riding, dog training, other activities with animals							
4. *Individual Competition Sports:* Wrestling or boxing, bowling, frisbee, tennis, archery, fencing, badminton, horseshoes, golf, pool or billiards, ping-pong							
5. *Team Sports:* Football, soccer, hockey, baseball, softball, basketball, volleyball, and the like							

	Compared to 5 years ago, I enjoy this activity:			I wish that this activity would occur:			Check if not applicable
SPORTS OR ATHLETIC ACTIVITIES (cont.)	LESS	SAME	MORE	LESS	SAME	MORE	
6. *Air Sports:* Piloting, gliding, parachuting							
7. *Snow Sports:* Skiing, sledding, snowmobiling							
8. Jogging or very fast walking							
9. Gymnastics							
10. Doing exercises fairly regularly							
11. Doing yoga							
12. Bicycling or motorcycling							
13. Ice skating or roller skating							
14. Going dancing							
15. Other:							
SPECTATOR ACTIVITIES							
1. Watching TV or listening to the radio							
2. Going to a sporting event							
3. Going to movies or plays							
4. Going to an X-rated movie							
5. Other:							
COMTEMPLATIVE AND SPIRITUAL ACTITIVIES							
1. Listening to records or music tapes							
2. Making time to be alone; enjoying solitude							
3. Reading the Scriptures							
4. Attending church							
5. Talking to God							
6. Hearing a good sermon							
7. Saying prayers							
8. Meditating							
9. Other:							

	Compared to 5 years ago, I enjoy this activity:			I wish that this activity would occur:			Check if not applicable
BEING WITH NATURE	LESS	SAME	MORE	LESS	SAME	MORE	
1. Listening to nature's sounds, such as the wind in the trees							
2. Looking at the sky, clouds, storms stars, sunrise, sunset							
3. Looking at flowers, plants, and trees							
4. Taking a drive into the country							
5. Walking or driving in the mountains							
6. Being at the ocean							
7. Spending time outdoors enjoying nature							
8. Going for a walk							
9. Other:							
SENSUOUS OR SELF-PLEASURING ACTIVITIES							
1. Being barefoot; feeling the earth with my feet							
2. Sun bathing; feeling the sun's warmth							
3. Sitting and thinking; daydreaming							
4. Napping							
5. Going without clothes, nude							
6. Singing or humming							
7. Buying something for myself							
8. Sleeping late in the morning							
9. Waking up early in the morning							
10. Masturbating							
11. Getting "high" on marijuana							
12. Having a drink or two							
13. Smoking							
14. Going to a spa or sauna bath							
15. Taking a hot, leisurely bath							

	Compared to 5 years ago, I enjoy this activity:			I wish that this activity would occur:			Check if not applicable
SENSUOUS OR SELF-PLEASURING ACTIVITIES (cont.)	LESS	SAME	MORE	LESS	SAME	MORE	
16. Going to a gym or health club							
17. Getting or giving a massage or backrub							
18. Other:							
EDUCATIONAL ACTIVITIES							
1. Going to a museum, exhibit, or library							
2. Learning something new							
3. Doing experiments or other scientific work							
4. Reading educational literature (technical, professional)							
5. Learning or speaking a foreign language							
6. Attending lectures, seminars, or taking a class							
7. Attending a concert (opera, dance, ballet, or rock festival)							
8. Other:							
GAMES OR PLAY ACTIVITIES							
1. Doing a crossword puzzle or solving a math problem							
2. Playing in snow, making a snowman, snow fights							
3. Spending time with animals; raising pets							
4. Playing bingo or cards							
5. Playing chess, checkers, scrabble, monopoly or other board games							
6. Other:							
GENERAL OR NONSPECIFIC PLEASURABLE ACTIVITIES							
1. Traveling							
2. Visiting a zoo, circus or amusement park							

	Compared to 5 years ago, I enjoy this activity:			I wish that this activity would occur:			Check if not applicable
GENERAL OR NONSPECIFIC PLEASURABLE ACTIVITIES (cont.)	LESS	SAME	MORE	LESS	SAME	MORE	
3. Exploring; hiking or walking in new places							
4. Gambling or betting							
5. Going to garage sales							
6. "People-watching"							
7. Planning vacations							
8. Reading for entertainment, such as a newspaper or novel							
9. Other:							

When was the last time you had "fun"? _____

_____

_____

_____

What were you doing? _____

_____

_____

_____

As you look back over the activities that you wish you did more frequently (column 2 of "Pleasurable Activities Questionnaire"), what *reasons* prevent you from doing so? _____

_____

_____

_____

_____

What kinds of things or activities do you do to relieve stress? _____

_____

_____

_____

Your reaction to this questionnaire:

Did you enjoy it?   Yes _____; Neutral _____; No _____

were adapted from similar scales by Zborowski (1962) and MacPhillamy and Lewinsohn (1976).

To discover which pleasurable activities mean something to you, try answering the questionnaire. The instructions are simple. For example, look at the first item: "Growing house-plants." How much pleasure do you receive from this activity now as compared to the past? If you still enjoy growing house-plants as much today as you did five years ago, place a check under SAME; if you enjoy this more, then place a check under MORE; if you enjoy the activity less, put your check under LESS. Then go to the second group of columns. What are your wishes for the future? If you wish to grow houseplants more in the future than you do now, check MORE; if you are doing as much as you wish, check SAME; if you wish to reduce this activity in the future, check LESS.

Check the last column, "Not Applicable," if an activity is something either that you are unable to do, that is not pleasurable, or that you have no interest in doing. Complete the questionnaire and reflect upon your answers before reading on.

The activities on the Pleasurable Activities Scale are classified into:

1. creative or self-expressive
2. giving service to others
3. work- or job-related activities
4. social involvement: family, friends, community
5. sports or athletic activities
6. spectator activities
7. contemplative and spiritual activities
8. being with nature
9. sensuous or self-pleasuring
10. educational activities
11. games or play activities
12. general or nonspecific pleasurable activities.

The scale can be used to analyze what general modality or types of pleasure are most important to an individual.

After you have completed the experiential exercise, look

carefully at your responses to see what they signify. Are you gaining the sort of enjoyment from life that you wish and that you are capable of having? Look at the individual categories. Is your enjoyment of educational activities or sports more than five years ago or less? Do you gain pleasure from spiritual involvements or from giving service to others as much as you want . . . or not? In what ways are you changing? In which categories of activities are you most involved? In which categories do you want to be most involved in the future? What can you do about improving your enjoyment of life? Keep in mind that it is up to you to locate the resources you wish and to learn how to use them. What have you learned about yourself through responding to this questionnaire?

If you find that your pleasures are more limited than they were five years ago, you are likely to blame forces seemingly outside your control. Perhaps your health isn't as good as it once was; perhaps your income is more limited, or inflation has reduced your standard of living; perhaps your sources of transportation are inadequate; perhaps some people close to you have died or moved away. All these circumstances may be true; they may be valid reasons for your difficulties in finding sources of pleasure.

The question that still arises, however, is that, given the limitations seemingly placed on you, what are *you* going to do? In the final analysis, you are the person most responsible for you, and others can only facilitate, support, or make things easier. It's amazing how many sources of pleasure you can find once you decide that you are going to look and that to do so is all right.

What happens to participation in pleasurable activities with aging? Some of my own work indicates a significant decrease in all areas: With rare exceptions, most older people stop anticipating or wishing for more pleasurable activities in the future. Few people report enjoyment of new activities with aging; and fun is strikingly infrequent. A 73-year-old retired man once told me, "I don't know what fun is—it was so long ago that I can't remember."

Part of the explanation for the general decrease of pleasurable activities with aging, I have found, is that most older people limit their types and sources of pleasure. Most older people find pleasure only in relating to others or in social activities. While socializing is certainly a vital part of life, it also means that losses often go unreplaced, leaving the person with a general emptiness and vulnerability to depression.

Too often we get locked into just a few activities, forgetting the variety of possible pleasures in life. With aging, markedly fewer activities are shared with a family. Unless the ability to find new pleasures is purposely nurtured, then the vacuum of time will be filled with boredom.

In summary, the greater the extent of pleasurable activities, the greater the older person's sense of well-being. Happiness has a positive relationship with the number of leisure-time activities enjoyed and the time spent in pleasurable activities (Fellow, 1956). However, we have never been taught how to pleasure and enjoy ourselves: Some people act as if they fear this unfamiliar state more than suffering.

THE PLEASURES OF AGING

The more sources of pleasure you enjoy, the happier you are (Fast, 1975). And the more ways you find of pleasuring, the greater your capacity for having pleasure. Pleasuring is like a muscle that needs to be exercised or it becomes weakened or useless.

On the whole, ". . . regardless of income, education, age, or retirement status [p. 307]," pleasure preferences are developed during middle age, are set at age 40, and remain consistent into old age (Zborowski, 1962, p. 307). Twenty centuries ago the philosopher Marcus Cicero wrote in his *De Senectute:*

> If one lives those earlier years narrowly or in terms of interests which can only be satisfied in youth, one must expect that old age will itself be narrow.

Making the most of your *entire* life, therefore, is the ultimate goal. Your values can be thus extremely important determinants of your thoughts, feelings, and lifestyle. Whatever your conclusion about values and the importance of pleasure, without your own original philosophy of life you can do no more than act out the conventional myths. Your power is in your dreams and, at the same time, in making each day a celebration. While no research sustains the following statement, I believe that more people die from lack of fulfillment and pleasure than from any other cause.

In fact, aging has undeniable advantages. Roberto Assagioli (1973), psychologist and philosopher, wrote that ". . . harmony, balance, and serenity mature in the older person and are the source of a tranquil but profound and lasting joy . . . . An older person can consciously re-evoke, resuscitate and cultivate in himself the positive characteristics of all his preceding ages [pp. 9-10]." And Henry Miller, writing at the age of 80, says:

> Perhaps the most comforting thing about growing old gracefully is the increasing ability not to take things too seriously. One of the big differences between a genuine sage and a preacher is gaiety . . . . I have lost many illusions, but fortunately not my enthusiasm, nor the joy of living, nor my unquenchable curiosity . . . . No matter how restricted my world may become I cannot imagine it leaving me void of wonder. In a sense, I suppose, it might be called my religion. I do not ask how it came about, this creation in which we swim, but only to enjoy and appreciate it. . . . Whatever I do. I do first for enjoyment.[3]

Our ordinary heroes and heroines of aging are similar to Assagioli and Miller in their ability to create advantages with aging, to continue growing, and to live life with enjoyment.

PLEASURE AND LIVING: A PERSONAL STATEMENT BY LIL

I started out adulthood looking for an absolute. I had wanted to find *the* answer, a principle to live by. I ardently longed for a

[3] *On Turning Eighty* (Santa Barbara: Capra Press, 1972), pp. 11-15.

tangible purpose and simple direction, in exchange for so many unanswerable questions about life.

But as the questions grew more perceptive, so did my awareness of the absence of absolutes. The meaning of life is in becoming aware of the inter-relationships and relativity of behaviors, decisions, events, tasks, ethics, meanings, and values. Every event is related to every other event. Meaning is to be found in inter-connectedness: The challenge is to reach for the many levels of understanding.

Viktor Frankl, in his excellent book *Man's Search for Meaning* (1963), says:

> Life ultimately means taking the responsibility to find the right answer to its problems and to fulfill the tasks which it constantly sets for each individual. These tasks, and therefore the meaning of life, differ from man to man, and from moment to moment. Thus it is impossible to define the meaning of life in a general way. *Questions about the meaning of life can never be answered by sweeping statements.* "Life" does not mean something vague, but something very real and concrete, just as life's tasks are also very real and concrete. They form man's destiny, which is different and unique for each individual.   *[p. 157]*

Today, a part of my being still craves absolutes. I will probably always search and wonder. However, the most positive times in my life have been when I fully realized that I am responsible for seeking my own truths and that my destiny is interwoven with my values—and I have many—none of which are absolute. For example, I value: creative risk-taking, security, gracefulness, differences, understanding, tolerance for ambiguity, clarity, balance and proportion, selfishness, selflessness, beauty, pleasure, suffering and pain and growth, openness, privacy, altruism, integrity, loyalty, authenticity, community building, relatedness with others—and most of all, love.

To love usually involves all of the other values. Perhaps because it involves so much is why the beauty and wonder of love have been sung by so many. And love is important at any age. Charles Chaplin, at 75, wrote:

> My life is more thrilling today than it ever was . . . . For the last twenty years I have known what happiness means. I have the good fortune to be married to a wonderful wife. I wish I could write more about this, but it involves love, and perfect love is the most beautiful of all frustrations because it is more than one can express.[4]

Love holds the deepest potential of fulfillment. It can of course also become distorted, unrelated to other behavior, twisted, and fanatical—but then so can every other human value and behavior. To live with a faith in love—despite hurts, losses, disappointments, and scars—is one of life's greatest challenges.

To me, the most pathetic, common complaint of older persons is that they feel useless. Their lives no longer feel valuable or meaningful. Such people, often retired, are lonely, bored, and spiritually unemployed. Without goals and striving, life becomes filled with despair, hopelessness, alienation, and passivity—no matter how much potential pleasure exists.

There has to be a world outside of the self. People who are obsessed with themselves are most afraid of age. Narcissism is spiritually sterile. A person, surrounded by pleasures, can still be miserable.

Any extremes of behavior, belief, or lifestyle are liable to become sterile as well as destructive. Sometimes, for example, older people put too much emphasis on religion, drawing energy away from the needs of the world. While religion can console the older person in his or her isolation and loss, and while it enables spiritual growth, it is distorted by some people into an egocentric withdrawal, as if the world's business is unimportant and mean.

Life is too often lived like a Greek tragedy that carries you along in a seemingly pre-written script. To write your own

---

[4] Morton Puner, *To the Good Long Life: What We Know about Growing Old* (New York: Universe, 1974), p. 271.

life script, you must constantly generate and recharge personal vitality. New goals must be found when old ones die, as we move toward our own death. Our energy must be redirected to uncover fresh meanings in life. We need to seek relationships with people rather than with things—intimacy, as well as productivity. A dynamic attitude toward life precludes retirement—in the true sense. *The search is for coherence among your personal undertakings and for the relation of your whole self to the rest of humanity.*

PLEASURE AND AGING:
A CONCLUDING THOUGHT

By itself, pleasure is a limited philosophical absolute. At one extreme, a life of pleasure without goals or meanings would fizzle out into empty satiations. At the other extreme, without the capacity for pleasure, life's meanings would be lifeless experiences; values would be merely intellectualized and compartmentalized. Pleasure is the experiential part of living. It resides in love, kindness, cooperation, discovery, achievement, games, fun, nature appreciation, and intelligence; it integrates the spiritual with physical vitality and excitement. Pleasure, when attached to meanings, gives substance to life's purposes. It can be the positive emotional experience of living values.

For the older person, as for everyone, pleasurable experiences are a necessity. Intelligent pleasure, along with the search for life meanings and ethical living, provide the substance for health and the energy to live. To spice our life with pleasure is as important as to season our food. "Pure" pleasure can open new dimensions of your self and the capacity for experiencing positives in life. When you enjoy life, you cherish it more.

People who have spent a lifetime giving to others or dedicated to productivity have to find new ways of living when they retire—if they want to continue living. My father never learned this lesson. He died the year of his retirement. We both knew he was going to die, long before his cancer appeared. And then, when he learned that he was sick, he hid the fact. He didn't want medical care; he wanted to die. He had worked hard all his life, dedicating it to others. Now his beloved children were grown and independent. His goals were accomplished. Retirement to him meant being locked in a prison in which nothing was left to do, nothing left to live for. His dying words were, "Learn to enjoy life . . . I never did . . ."

Goals, incentives, life meanings, purposes—these are creative quests that never end. Our nobility lies not only in the courage to be, but in the courage to become. My personal heroes are those who refuse the premature death due to a feeling of being unwanted and unnecessary. They find new relationships to the world as they rise above their losses and suffering.

Neugarten (1972) indicates that a "high life satisfaction is more often present in older persons who are socially active and involved than in persons who were inactive and uninvolved [p. 11]." But the older person in America is often faced with a limited range of goals from which to choose, because of discrimination against older persons. Nevertheless, with courage and preparation, aging can be an opportunity to share ourselves with others at a time when we are free of work tensions. Growing older can be a period of stretching out to new interests. It can be our chance to energetically involve ourselves with social needs. It can also mean being left with the ultimate search of finding ourselves, our relationship to others, and our connection to the universe. At the age of 80, Bertrand Russell, English philosopher and champion of individual liberty, wrote:

> Psychologically, there are two dangers to be guarded against in old age. One of these is undue absorption with the past . . . . The other thing to be avoided is clinging to youth in the hope of sucking vigor from vitality . . . . The best way to overcome it—so at least it seems to me—is to make your interests gradually wider and more im-

personal, until bit by bit the walls of the ego recede and your life becomes increasingly merged in the universal life. An individual human existence should be like a river—small at first, narrowly contained within its banks, and rushing passionately . . . . Gradually, the river grows wider, the banks recede, the waters flow more quietly, and in the end, without any visible break, they become merged in the sea.[5]

[5] Puner, *To the Good Long Life,* pp. 271–72.

BIBLIOGRAPHY

Aakster, C. W. Psycho-social stress and health disturbances. *Social Science and Medicine,* February 1974, *8,* 77–90.

Aronoff, C. Old age in prime time. *Journal of Communication,* 1974, *24,* 86–87.

Ashmore, S. Commercial television's calculated indifference to the old. *The Center Magazine,* March/April 1975, *8,* 18–21.

Assagioli, R. *The conflict between the generations and the psychosynthesis of the human ages.* New York: Psychosynthesis Research Foundation, Inc., 1973, Issue No. 31.

Bachtold, M. & E. Werner. Personality profiles of women psychologists: Three generations. *Developmental Psychology,* 1971, *5*:2, 273–278.

Bahr, R. Activity will keep you young. *Prevention,* May 1972, 100–107.

Balint, M. *Problems of human pleasure and behavior.* New York: Liveright Publications Corporation, 1956.

Baltes, P. B. & K. W. Schaie. Aging and IQ: The myth of the twilight years. *Psychology Today,* March 1974, *7,* 35–40.

Barry, A. J. *et al.* The effects of physical conditioning on older individuals. *Journal of Gerontology*, 1966, *21*, 182–191.

Belloc, N. Relationship of health practices and mortality. *Preventive Medicine*, 1973, *2*, 67–81.

Belknap, M. M., R. A. Blau, and R. N. Grossman. *Case studies and methods in humanistic medical care.* San Francisco, Calif.: Institute for the Study of Humanistic Medicine, 1975.

Bennett, R. and J. Eckman. Attitudes toward aging: A critical examination of recent literature and implications for future research. In C. Eisdorfer and M. Lawton (eds.), *The psychology of adult development and aging.* Washington, D.C.: American Psychological Association, 1973.

Blanchard, E. and L. Young. Self-control of cardiac functioning. *Psychological Bulletin*, March 1973, *79*, 145–163.

Blum, J. E., L. F. Jarvik, and E. T. Clark. Rate of change on selective tests of intelligence: A twenty-year longitudinal study of aging. *Journal of Gerontology*, 1970, *25*:3, 171–176.

Bolen, J. S. Meditation and psychotherapy in the treatment of cancer. *Psychic*, July/August 1973, 19–22.

Botwinick, J. *Aging and behavior.* New York: Springer Publishing Company, 1973.

Boyd, R. and C. Oakes. *Foundations of practical gerontology.* Columbia, S.C.: University of South Carolina Press, 1969.

Brenneis, C. B. Older women are less afraid and worried than younger women. *Science News*, 1975, *108*, 361–2.

Bricklin, M. Must women protect their hearts? *Prevention*, December 1973, 134–145.

Bridges, W. The discovery of middle age. *Human Behavior*, May 1977, *6*, 65–68.

Butler, R. N. The destiny of creativity in later life: Studies of creative people and the whole creative process. In S. Levin and R. J. Kahana (eds.), *Psychodynamic studies on aging.* New York: International Universities Press, 1967.

———. The life review: an interpretation of reminiscence in the aged. In B. Neugarten (ed.), *Middle age and aging,* Chicago: University of Chicago Press, 1968, 486–496.

——— and M. I. Lewis. *Aging and mental health.* St. Louis: C. V. Mosby Co., 1973.

Cameron, P. Ego strength and happiness of the aged. *Journal of Gerontology*, 1967, *22*, 199–202.

———. Mood as an indicant of happiness: Age, sex, social class and situational differences. *Journal of Gerontology*, 1975, *30*:2, 216–224.

Camus, A. *The myth of Sisyphus.* New York: Vintage Books, 1955.

Cleveland, W. and D. Gianturco. Remarriage probability after widowhood: A retrospective method. *Journal of Gerontology,* 1976, *31:*1, 99–103.

Collier, B. Fight retirement, enjoy sex and don't become "A wrinkled baby." *People Magazine,* November 1975, 29–32.

Comfort, A. *The process of aging.* New York: The New American Library, 1961.

Cooley, L. and L. Cooley. *How to avoid the retirement trap.* New York: Popular Library, 1972.

Cooper, M. and K. H. Cooper. *Aerobics for women.* New York: M. Evans & Co., 1972.

Corsini, R. J. and K. K. Fassett. Intelligence and aging. *The Journal of Genetic Psychology,* 1953, *83,* 249–264.

Craig, M. *21-day shape-up program.* New York: Random House, 1968.

Craik, F. I. M. Age differences in human memory. In J. E. Birren and K. W. Schaie (eds.), *Handbook of the psychology of aging.* New York: Van Nostrand Reinhold, 1977, 384–420.

Dangott, L. R. Stereotypes of aging. Slide study of aging and popular advertising. Reno: University of Nevada, 1975a.

———. Pleasurable activities: Age related changes. Reno: University of Nevada, 1975b (mimeographed).

———. "Grief and mourning: Dynamics in psychotherapy." Paper read at the Western Gerontological Society conference, March 1976, San Diego, Calif.

Davis, R. H. Television communication and the elderly. In D. S. Woodruff and J. E. Birren (eds.), *Aging: Scientific perspectives and social issues.* New York: Van Nostrand Reinhold, 1975.

de Beauvoir, S. *The coming of age.* New York: Warner Library, 1973.

de Castillejo, I. *Knowing woman.* New York: Harper & Row, 1973.

Dill, D. V. and K. Wasserman. Fitness at age 90: A new record. *The Gerontologist,* 1964, *4,* 136–140.

Eisdorfer, C. Resources for the aged reflect strongly held social myths. *The Center Magazine,* March 1975, *8,* 12–18.

Elwell, C. C. The image of cancer. *Human Behavior,* August 1975, *4,* 41–43.

Emhart, B. Taming the wild spine. *Prevention,* December 1973, 121–132.

Esquire Magazine. How to get old and do it right. April 1975, 73–76.

Fast, J. *The pleasure book.* New York: Stein & Day, 1975.

Fellows, E. W. A study of factors related to happiness. *Journal of Educational Research,* 1956, *50,* 231–234.

Fengler, A. P. and V. Wood. The generation gap: An analysis of attitudes of contemporary issues. *The Gerontologist,* Summer 1972, Pt. 1, *12,* 124–128.

Fillenbaum, G. G. On the relations between attitude to work and attitude to retirement. *Journal of Gerontology,* 1971, *26:*2, 244–248.

Fletcher, J. Being happy, being human. *The Humanist,* January 1975, *35,* 13–15.

Frankl, Viktor. *Man's search for meaning: An introduction to Logotherapy.* New York: Washington Square Press, 1963.

Frazier, K. Science and the parascience cults. *Science News,* May 29, 1976, *109* (22), 346–350.

Freedman, J. and P. Shaver. What makes you happy? *Psychology Today,* October 1975, *9,* 66–72.

Gerber, I., R. Rusalem, N. Hannon, D. Battin, and A. Arkin. Anticipatory grief and aged widows and widowers. *Journal of Gerontology,* 1975, *30,* 225–229.

Glamser, F. Determinants of a positive attitude toward retirement. *Journal of Gerontology,* 1976, *31:*1, 104–107.

Golde, P. and N. Kogan. A sentence completion procedure for assessing attitudes toward old people. *Journal of Gerontology,* 1959, *14,* 355–363.

Goleman, D. Meditation helps break the stress spiral. *Psychology Today,* February 1976, *9,* 82–93.

Goudy, W. J., E. A. Powers, and P. Keith. Work and retirement: A test of attitudinal relationships. *Journal of Gerontology,* 1975, *30:*2, 193–198.

Harris, L., and Associates. The myth and reality of aging in America. Washington, D.C.: National Council on the Aging, 1975.

Havinghurst, R. J. Successful aging. *The Gerontologist,* March 1961, *1,* 8–13.

Hayflick, L. Why grow old? *The Stanford Magazine,* 1975, 36–43.

Hoffer, A. Senility is a form of chronic malnutrition. In L. Summit (ed.), *The crisis in health care for the aging.* New York: The Huxley Institute, 1972.

Holmes, T. H. and R. H. Rahe. The social readjustment rating scale. *Journal of Psychosomatic Research,* 1967, *11,* 213–218.

Human Behavior. The muscle reviver. January 1976, *5,* 38–39.

Johnson, J. What doctors don't know about reducing. *Prevention,* May 1973, 146–158.

Jonas, G. *Visceral learning.* New York: Pocket Books, 1974.

Jourard, S. *The transparent self.* New York: Van Nostrand Reinhold, 1964.

Jung, C. G. *Modern man in search of a soul.* New York: Harcourt, Brace & World, 1933.

Kalish, R. A. Death and dying in a social context. In R. Binstock and E. Shanas (eds.), *Handbook of aging and the social sciences.* New York: Van Nostrand Reinhold, 1976, 483–507.

Kalish, R. A. and D. K. Reynolds. *Death and ethnicity: A psychocultural study.* Los Angeles: University of Southern California Press, 1976.

Kaluger, G. and M. Kaluger. *Human development: The span of life.* St. Louis, Mo.: C. V. Mosby Co., 1974.

Kastenbaum, R. J. (ed.) *Psycho-biology of aging.* New York: Springer Publishing Co., 1965.

———. *Death, society and human experience.* St. Louis: C. V. Mosby Co., 1977.

Keen, S. An interview with Dr. Elisabeth Kubler-Ross. *Family Circle,* September 1975, 44–46, 51.

———. Ivan Illich: Medicine is a major threat to health. *Psychology Today,* May 1976, *9*, 66–67.

Keen, S. and A. V. Fox. *Telling your story.* New York: Doubleday, 1973.

Kimmel, D. C. *Adulthood and aging.* New York: John Wiley & Sons, 1974.

Kramer, C. H., J. Kramer, and H. E. Dunlop. Resolving grief. *Geriatric Nursing,* July–August 1966, 14–17.

Kuntzleman, C. (ed.) *The physical fitness encyclopedia.* Emmans, Penn.: Rodale Books, 1971.

Lawton, M. P. Ecology and aging. In L. Pastalan and D. Carson (eds.) *Spatial behavior of older people.* Ann Arbor: University of Michigan–Wayne State University Institute of Gerontology, 1970.

Leaf, A. Getting old. *Scientific American,* September 1973, *229:*3, 44–53.

———. *Youth in old age.* New York: McGraw-Hill Book Company, 1975.

LeShan, L. *How to meditate: A guide to self-discovery.* Boston: Little, Brown & Co., 1974.

Levine, S. Stress and behavior. *Scientific American,* January 1971, *224:*1, 26–31.

Lewis, C. N. Reminiscing and self-concept in old age. *Journal of Gerontology,* 1971, *26:*2, 240–243.

———. The adaptive value of reminiscing in old age. *Journal of Geriatric Psychiatry,* 1973, *6:*1, 117–121.

Lowen, A. *Pleasure.* New York: Coward-McCann, Inc., 1970.

———. *Bioenergetics.* New York: Coward-McCann, Inc., 1975.

Lurie, J. and S. Segev. (eds.) *The Israel army physical fitness book.* New York: Grosset & Dunlap, 1969.

Lynch, D. J. Future time perspective and impulsivity in old age. *Journal of Genetic Psychology,* 1971, *118,* 245–252.

Maas, H. and J. Kuypers. *From thirty to seventy.* San Francisco: Jossey-Bass, Inc., 1974.

MacFarland, R. A. The sensory and perceptual processes in aging. In K. W. Schaie (ed.), *Theory and methods of research on aging.* Morgantown, W. Va.: West Virginia University Press, 1968.

MacPhillamy, D. J. and P. M. Lewinsohn. Manual for the pleasant events schedule. University of Oregon, 1976, mimeograph.

Maddox, G. L. Adaptation to retirement. *The Gerontologist,* Spring 1970 (Pt. 2), *10,* 14–18.

Maness, B. What you don't know about exercise. *Reader's Digest,* April 1976, 129–131.

Marcus, R. Retired person's groups: Loneliness and fear; Giving and growth. *Voices, the art and science of psychotherapy,* Summer 1974, *10,* 35–40.

Martin, E. Why Europeans get more fun out of life than Americans. *National Enquirer,* July 6, 1976, 19.

Maslow, A. *Toward a psychology of being.* New York: D. Van Nostrand Co., 1962.

Masters, W. H. and V. E. Johnson. *Human sexual response.* Boston: Little, Brown & Co., 1966.

—— *Human sexual inadequacy.* Boston: Little, Brown & Co., 1970.

McMahon, A. and P. Rhudick. Reminiscing in the aged: An adaptational response. In S. Levin (ed.) *Psychodynamic studies on aging.* New York: International Universities Press, 1967.

Merton, R. A social psychological factor. In A. M. Rose (ed.) *Race prejudice and discrimination.* New York: Alfred Knopf, 1951.

Metropolitan Life Insurance Statistical Bulletin, Longevity of corporate executives. February 1974, *55,* 1–3.

Miller, N. Learning of visceral and glandular responses. *Science,* 1969, *163,* 434–445.

Mischel, W. Continuity and change in personality. *American Psychologist,* 1969, *24,* 1,012–1,018.

Morehouse, L. *Total fitness.* New York: Simon & Schuster, 1975.

——. Personality and the aging process. *The Gerontologist,* Spring, 1972, *12,* 9–15.

——. Personality and aging. In J. E. Birren and K. W. Schaie (eds.) *Handbook of the psychology of aging.* New York: Van Nostrand Reinhold, 1977, pp. 626–649.

Neugarten, B. L., R. J. Havinghurst, and S. S. Tobin. Personality and patterns of aging. In Neugarten, B. L. (ed.) *Middle age and aging.* Chicago: University of Chicago Press, 1968.

Neulinger, J. and C. Raps. Leisure attitudes of an intellectual elite. *Journal of Leisure Research,* 1972, 4:3, 196–207.

Palmore, E. B. Predicting longevity: A follow-up controlling for age. *Gerontologist,* Winter 1969, *9,* 247–250.

——. The effects of aging on activities and attitudes. In V. Brantl and M. R. Brown (eds.) *Readings in Gerontology.* St. Louis: C. V. Mosby Co., 1973.

Palmore, E. B. and K. Manton. Ageism compared to racism and sexism. *Journal of Gerontology,* 1973, *28:*3, 363–369.

Parkes, C. M. *Bereavement.* New York: International Universities Press, 1972.

Peterson, D. Life-span education and gerontology. *The Gerontologist,* October 1975, *15,* 436–441.

Peterson, J. Leisure without guilt. In V. Boyack (ed.) *Time on our hands: The problem of leisure.* Los Angeles: Andrus Gerontology Center Publishing Center, USC, 1973.

—— and B. Payne. *Love in the later years: The emotional, physical, sexual and social potential of the elderly.* New York: Association Press, 1975.

Popov, I. *Stay young.* New York: Grosset & Dunlap, 1975.

Powell, R. R. and R. H. Pohndorf. Comparison of adult exercisers and nonexercisers on fluid intelligence and selected physiological variables. *The Research Quarterly,* 1971, *42:*1, 70–77.

Preston, C. Behavior modification: A therapeutic approach to aging and dying. *Postgraduate Medicine,* December 1973, *54:*6, 64–68.

Rahe, R. H., M. Meyer, M. Smith, G. Kjaer, and T. H. Holmes. Social stress and illness onset. *Journal of Psychosomatic Research,* 1964, *8,* 35–44.

—— and E. Lind. Psychosocial factors and sudden cardiac death: A pilot study. *Journal of Psychosomatic Research,* 1971, *15,* 19–24.

Redmond, D. P., M. S. Gaylor, R. H. McDonald, and A. P. Shapiro. Blood pressure and heart-rate response to verbal instruction and relaxation in hypertension. *Psychosomatic Medicine,* July 1974, *36,* 285–297.

Riegel, K. F. and R. M. Riegel, Development, drop, and death. *Developmental Psychology,* 1972, *6,* 306–319.

Riley, M., A. Foner, and associates. *Aging and society: Vol. 1.* New York: Russell Sage Foundation, 1968.

Roberts, J. L., L. R. Kimsey, D. O. Logan, and G. Shaw. How aged in nursing homes view dying and death. *Geriatrics,* April 1970, *25,* 115–119.

Rosenzweig, M. R. and E. L. Bennett. Enriched environments: Facts, factors, fantasies. In J. McGaugh and L. Petrinovich (eds.) *Knowing, thinking, and believing.* New York: Plenum Press, 1976.

Ross, E. K. *On death and dying.* New York: Macmillan, 1969.

Rothenberg, R. *Health in the later years.* New York: New American Library, 1964.

Royal Canadian Air Force (RCAF). *Exercise plans for physical fitness.* Canada: Crown Publishers, 1962.

Samuels, M. and N. Samuels. *Seeing with the mind's eye.* New York: Random House, 1975.

Saul, S. *Aging: An album of people growing old.* New York: John Wiley & Sons, 1974.

Schiffman, S. S. Taste and smell changes of foods during the aging process. *The Gerontologist,* October 1975, *15,* 56 (abstract).

Science News. Less stress in traditional Japan. August 23, 1975a, *108,* 216.

———. Can brain damage be overcome? November 15, 1975b, *108,* 313.

———. Cancer: Who gets it? Risk groups reported. January 1976, *109,* 69.

Seltzer, M. M. and R. C. Atchley. The concept of old: Changing attitudes and stereotypes. *The Gerontologist,* Autumn (Pt. 1) 1971, *11,* 226–230.

Selye, H. Stress and aging. *Journal of the American Geriatric Society,* September 1970, *9,* 669–680.

———. *Stress without distress.* Philadelphia: J. B. Lippincott Co., 1974.

Shanas, E. Health and adjustment in retirement. *The Gerontologist,* Spring 1970, *10,* 19–21.

Silverman, S. *How will you feel tomorrow? New ways to predict illness.* New York: Stein & Day, 1973.

Slater, P. Sexual adequacy in America. *Intellectual Digest,* November 1973, 17–20.

Smith, T. L. *The Shangri-La effect: Inducing aging-like behavior in college students.* Presentation at the International Congress of Gerontology, Kiev, USSR, 1975.

Stein, J. *Effective personality: A humanistic approach.* Belmont, Calif.: Wadsworth Publishing Co., 1972.

Sutich, A. and M. Vich (eds.) *Readings in humanistic psychology.* New York: The Free Press, 1969.

Sviland, M. A. Helping elderly people become sexually liberated: Psychosocial issues. *Counseling Psychologist,* 1975, *5:*1, 67–72.

Szasz, T. S. *Pain and pleasure, a study of bodily feelings.* New York: Basic Books, 1957.

Taylor, R. *Hunza health secrets.* New York: Award Books, 1964.

Tissue, T. Disengagement potential: Replication and use as an explanatory variable. *Journal of Gerontology,* 1971, *26:*1, 76–80.

———. Old age and the perception of poverty. *Sociology and Social Research,* 1971–2, *56,* 331–344.

Townsend, C. *Old age, the last segregation.* New York: Bantam Books, 1971.

USDHEW, *Working with Older People, Vol. I: The Practitioner and the Elderly.* Washington, D.C.: Government Printing Office, 1966.

Wallace, R. K. and H. Benson. The physiology of meditation. *Scientific American,* February 1972, *226,* 84–90.

Waxler, S. H. *Current therapy.* New York: W. B. Saunders, 1971.

White, R. B. and L. T. Gathman. The syndrome of ordinary grief. *American Family Practitioner*, August 1973, *8*, 97–104.

Wilkie, F. and C. Eisdorfer. Intelligence and blood pressure in the aged. *Science*, May 1971, *172*, 959–962.

Wilmot, S. S. *Dyadic communication: A transactional perspective*. Cambridge, Mass.: Addison-Wesley Publishing, 1975.

Wilson, W. Correlates of avowed happiness. *Psychological Bulletin*, 1967, *67:*4, 294–306.

Winter, R. *Ageless aging*. New York: Crown Publishers, 1973.

Wood, V. Age-appropriate behavior for older people. *The Gerontologist*, Winter 1971 (Part II), *11*, 74–78.

Woodruff, D. S. Introduction: Multidisciplinary perspectives of aging. In D. S. Woodruff and J. E. Birren (eds.) *Aging: Scientific perspectives and social issues*. New York: Van Nostrand Reinhold, 1975a.

——. A physiological perspective of the psychology of aging. In D. S. Woodruff and J. E. Birren (eds.) *Aging: Scientific perspectives and social issues*. New York: Van Nostrand Reinhold, 1975b.

Zborowski, M. Aging and recreation. *Journal of Gerontology*, 1962, *17*, 302–309.

INDEX